A Yak
for Christmas

Louise Hillary is also the author of

KEEP CALM IF YOU CAN

A Yak
for Christmas

BY LOUISE HILLARY

GARDEN CITY, NEW YORK

DOUBLEDAY & COMPANY, INC.

1969

Contents

1. Innocents Abroad 1
2. Katmandu at Last 17
3. Into the Khumbu 29
4. A Hospital for the Sherpas 44
5. Sherpa Hospitality 52
6. Traders, Snow Leopards, and Temba 64
7. Fun at Phortse 72
8. The Hospital Opening 88
9. On the Way to Everest 100
10. Base Camp Conquered 118
11. Christmas in Sherpaland 134
12. A Yak for Father Christmas 148
13. Trekking to Solu 157
14. Village of the Moon 172
15. Down to Earth 191
16. The King's Road 208
17. First-Class Gents 227
18. Farewell Himalayas 245

CHAPTER 1

Innocents Abroad

....

The Ambassador looked slightly pained. He had been en-joying ten minutes of much needed peace and privacy sitting in a comfortable chair in the VIP lounge of the Auckland Airport, and now into this restful seclusion came eight persons, not very important, but very excited: two mothers and six noisy children about to depart on a holiday.

The telephone rang for His Excellency, and while he was occupied we made a dive for cups of coffee and talked at the tops of our voices. Every so often the Ambassador gave us a despairing glance, obviously vowing never to be trapped in a VIP lounge again. A look of considerable relief spread over his face when the loudspeaker announced the plane for Hong Kong. He made a hasty and rather undignified exit toward the aircraft, and the eight of us followed in joyous anticipation.

We were undoubtedly a well-dressed and well-prepared group, I thought. Everyone was wearing new clothes of the kind that would drip dry and not show the dirt, and each person had an airways bag crammed with necessities for the voyage—a set of snakes and ladders, a box of chocolates, a very powerful magnet, a sheath knife, a couple of

bottles of aspirins, and a ukulele—all important requirements on a flight to Hong Kong.

The fathers of our two families were thousands of miles
away in the Mount Everest region of Nepal. My husband,
Ed Hillary, had taken an expedition there to build a hospital for the Sherpa people, and Dr. Max Pearl was his
deputy leader. The two families had decided that once the
school examinations for the year were completed we would
join our husbands in Sherpaland for the Christmas holi-
days and camp and trek in the Himalayan mountains. So
here I was on November 30, 1966, heading for Hong Kong
with Peter, aged twelve; Sarah aged ten; Belinda, seven;
together with Lois Pearl and her three daughters: Ann,
fourteen; Lynn, twelve; and Susan, ten.

We waved good-bye to the lovely green fields and precipitous coast of New Zealand and flew out over the toss-
ing waters of the Tasman Sea. It was a long tiring day
before our jet descended toward Hong Kong. We had expected to find warm temperatures and soft breezes, but as
we approached the runway our plane was violently buf-
feted up and down and when we finally disembarked there
was a howling, cold gale. Thankful for our thick Himalayan jackets, we proceeded to the airport building. To our
surprise we were met by members of the press, who wanted
us to smile for photographs, even though we weren't in the
mood for smiles and photos. By the time they finished and
we had changed some money, we had missed the bus that
should have taken us to the city. We stood out in the cold
wind waiting for nearly half an hour until the bus returned to pick us up and deposit us at our hotel.

It was wonderful really to be in Hong Kong and to
sense something of the mystery of China. Lois had visited
Hong Kong before, but none of the rest of us had. What
a pity it was that we had to waste precious time by having
a few hours of sleep.

The hotel staff looked as though they were ready to go to bed for the night. When we asked for our rooms they seemed a little bit noncommittal. Finally we were shown two rooms with four beds for the eight of us. The children were tired after the excitement of the departure and they needed a good sleep. It was 2 A.M. in the morning by New Zealand time—rather late for children aged from seven to fourteen, and for their mothers.

I rang the telephone and various other bells I could see around the room, hoping that someone would come and help us. At last a sweet and utterly oriental gentleman appeared and said he would bring more beds. We put our four youngest to bed and then waited hopefully. Half an hour later we were feeling slightly desperate. Then two beds arrived for Lois, who settled her family and went and had a refreshing shower. I sat with my eldest child, who was doing his best to be philosophical about life and trying to appear wide awake and grown up. After another half hour of waiting, the little man at last returned with two more beds.

When he had gone and we had prepared the beds, I noticed a smoky smell coming in through the door. At first I ignored it, until I heard some fire engines shrieking along the street below. I poked my nose outside the door. To my amazement I saw smoke billowing out of a ventilator in the corridor.

"That's us on fire. Good heavens!" What on earth do two mums and six kids, all in their nighties, do now?

I rushed to the window and to my horror saw in the street below three fire engines, two ambulances, and two police cars with red lights flashing alarmingly on their roofs. We were on the eighth floor, which was much too far away from ground level for jumping. Rather furtively I sneaked out into the corridor, where I found other hotel guests, all looking decidedly nervous.

When our pleasant little Chinese friend appeared, we asked his advice.

"Oh, it is all right," he said. "If anything was wrong I would tell you."

"Well, I think something is wrong," I said.

"That is all right," he replied in his happy singsong voice. "I will tell you."

I decided to have a talk with Lois.

Lois was looking very sleepy, but also very worried, as we stood by the window and discussed what to do. In addition to our six precious children we had a lot of important trekking equipment we were taking to the Himalayas. In our baffled and exhausted state this almost seemed the more important to us, for we had taken so much trouble in the last few months to collect our tough walking boots and countless items of warm clothing.

"Shall we throw all the luggage out of the window and then run for the nearest elevator?" I suggested. Lois agreed that maybe this was the best thing to do. Then another thought struck me. By the time we had thrown the luggage out of the window and reached the street it would all be stolen, so what was the use of that? We stood and wondered for another half hour. Then, as there were no new developments and no one, including the telephone operator, could tell us anything, we decided to give up and go to sleep.

I woke next morning about 5 A.M. with a terrible cold. My nose and eyes wouldn't stop streaming. In spite of that, it was exciting to look out the windows across to the island of Hong Kong and see the busy waterway crowded with large ships, ferries, junks, and every other kind of boat imaginable. There was still a stiff breeze, and, much to our surprise when we opened the windows, it was quite a cold day. We sat and absorbed Hong Kong with intense pleasure. Both families industriously wrote up their diaries, and I wondered to myself how long this enthusiasm would last.

That day we were shown the sights by two kind friends who were thoroughly understanding sorts, with young children of their own. After the invigorating experience of negotiating the busy and wind-whipped waters between Kowloon and Hong Kong by ferry, we did most of our sightseeing on double-decker trams and buses, which was an adventure in itself. Our party of ten had to negotiate the busy roads, with traffic streaming around, and often half the party would be clambering on a bus about to depart while the rest of us would be left stranded wondering what on earth to do.

One tram deposited us at Wanchai. This was our children's first experience of a really crowded area of humanity. It's an extraordinarily gay and busy place with colorful Chinese signs and laundry hanging out on long poles, and it was crowded with outdoor markets at this early hour of the morning. We could hardly move in the street. But later, we had to give up trying to keep the families together and only hoped that if we stopped about every twenty yards we could gather once more and then sally forth again. The merchandise in the markets was fascinating—"hundred-year-old" eggs and fatty pork sausages, and vivid green bundles of fresh vegetables.

We wandered through places where the houses were built on stilts on the edge of the water. I had never seen so much filth as was in between the houses, which were ramshackle affairs, made of anything the owners could find. But the owners themselves were shining and clean and their children immaculate in navy and white school uniforms. Everywhere we went we were impressed by the cleanliness and brightness of the people, who must find it difficult to keep up their standards when they live under such conditions.

We visited the Peak, of course, the high mountain lookout which stands as an everlasting craggy backdrop to the teeming life of this overcrowded city. When our cable car deposited us at the summit, I scrambled onto terra firma as quickly as possible, for the journey had reminded me of a bobsled ride I once took down the slopes of the Disneyland Matterhorn. There was a lovely soft hazy coloring about the view that one often associates with China—ethereal and very exquisite. Looking down over the city of Hong Kong and Kowloon was in itself worth the trip from New Zealand. The great throbbing city with its central area of shining white skyscrapers is a brilliant sight, and the impossibly narrow strip of concrete that is the international airport, running out into the harbor, made me shudder at the thought of the takeoff to Delhi that afternoon.

Like all foreign tourists to Hong Kong we had to buy some of the duty-free commodities. My cold was so bad that I was in no condition to do anything that required concentration, but we felt that we must go into at least one shop and see the prices. Also, I had been commissioned by my husband to buy a tripod for his large 16mm movie camera. Our friends took us to a reputable shop, where I proceeded to sneeze so violently that I could hardly see, let alone think. To the astonishment of the salesman I bought the first tripod he showed me, paid for it quickly, and hurried away as speedily as was humanly possible.

One short day in Hong Kong was not nearly enough, and we were sad as we drove out to the airport in the hotel minibus, with our great pile of Himalayan equipment insecurely tied to the roof rack. When we arrived at the airport we were welcomed by two BOAC airline officials, who took over our children, our baggage, our hand baggage, our passports, and us. It was like a dream. They led us to an elegant VIP lounge, where we were plied with cool drinks and pleasant conversation, and the children found a jug of pure, freshly squeezed orange juice and drank the lot.

There was panic when we discovered that everyone had to pay airport dues, as by this time we had no local money left. I am sure this happens to most travelers here, and we desperately dipped into bags and purses until we scraped together various types of foreign currency to get ourselves out of the place. Then our two protectors, carrying all our odds and ends, led us to the steps of the aircraft and saw us safely on our way to Delhi. We were sorry to see them go, for now Lois and I would have to look after ourselves.

The great jets roared into action, and as the plane rushed forward I felt akin to a luckless sailor of olden times who was being forced to walk the plank. (Seen from a distance the Hong Kong Airport runway bears a close resemblance to "the plank.") The down-to-earth chatter of the children soon woke me from my reverie and I realized we were comfortably airborne. Later, much to my surprise, the noise from the children faded away. They were exhausted, and they slept right through their meal—the only time this occurred during the two months' trip.

Our luxurious treatment in Hong Kong was not repeated in Delhi. It was late at night by the time we had cleared the Indian Customs. We managed to get all our luggage into one pile and found that a bus could take us directly to the hotel. We loaded our bags and ourselves into the bus and then waited inside for twenty minutes. When the children began to be restless, I searched through the deserted airport building and managed to find the driver. I asked if he could take us to the hotel.

"Oh, yes," he said, "when everybody else is ready we'll go."

A quarter of an hour later the ground hostess and an Indian official piled into the bus and the driver decided to proceed. The hostess and the official sat close up to the driver and talked and screamed with laughter. The driver, in fact, was so busy talking and laughing that he cut corners and drove in the middle of the road. As we were in a large vehicle I felt, with any luck, we would survive a collision.

We arrived safely at our rather modest hotel and were conducted to our rooms. Our one ambition was to go to sleep, but then we discovered that one family had only two beds and the other three. Why was it that despite prior and explicit bookings we seemed destined never to have enough beds? If this happened during the day, it would be funny, but somehow, at this time of night, it just didn't seem madly humorous.

Once again we waited a half hour for extra beds. I called the office downstairs.

"Really, can't you do something?" I said plaintively.

"I am sorry, madam," was the reply, "the bearer was sent to bring you an extra bed not so long ago, but on the way down, carrying the bed, he fell and cut his head very badly and is now having stitches in it. I am very sorry but we will send a replacement as soon as possible." Finally a bed appeared and the two bearers brought two cot mattresses to put on it. I wanted to push the men out of the room and fix the bed myself, for they spent ten minutes just trying to decide whether to put the cot mattresses across the bed, or longways, or one longways and one across. I stood there boiling with rage, waiting for them to make their momentous decision. At last they decided on the T shape—one longways and one across—and then I helped them put on the sheets and make up the bed.

Poor India! It is an inefficient country in many ways. The hotel we were in was a fine building, yet the telephone broke in my hand, and the toilet flushed only to let the water come out on the floor instead of into the bowl and we had a continuous flood. The food was quite good on the whole, but there weren't large amounts of it, and the butter was exactly like slightly rancid white fat. We all had a guilty feeling eating as much food as we did. We consoled ourselves with the thought that at least as tourists we were bringing much needed money into the country.

It's amazing what a good night's sleep can do. By morning we felt fresh and ready for a day of looking around Delhi. Our hotel was in the central area and it was easy to walk to a large bazaar nearby. The children were enthralled with all the colorful objects and bought little trinkets for just a few pennies. Everyone took photographs and bargained with fruit vendors, watched the snake charmer, and then went on a tour. At the end of the day we returned to the hotel filled with enthusiasm and happiness, with leis around our necks, red Hindu dots on our foreheads, and bursting with information about India.

I have been lucky enough to have done a lot of traveling, but the one thing I never seem to manage is to be a real down-to-earth tourist with cameras round my neck. And maybe a free and easy feeling of no hurry. This time I was determined to be a tourist and go on a two-day trip to Agra and its surrounding places of interest, so we hired two cars and two drivers and set forth very early one morning.

Traveling by car through the Indian countryside is hard work but great fun, and our two drivers were only too happy to stop whenever we asked. We had one unscheduled stop because of a puncture. I mentioned that it might be a good idea if we had the tire fixed, but no one seemed particularly interested. We stopped for the children to

have an elephant ride and we stopped again for them to
see brickmaking, oxen turning water wheels, performing
bears, camels, and countless other things. It was all a marvelous lighthearted traveling geography lesson.

Our party was to stay at the delightful and dignified
Lawries Hotel in Agra. We had two lovely rooms for the
two families and, believe it or not, two beds for the four
Hillarys and two beds for the four Pearls! We just looked
at each other, speechless, and laughed. I must say that on
this occasion the beds were brought promptly; as Peter
had a strong feeling about the lack of beds by now, he
helped the bearers carry them down the passageway and
install them safely in our rooms. Since Lawries Hotel was
built in the grand old days of the British Raj, my bedroom
was about the size of my whole house at home, and beyond the bedroom was a spacious room and a large bathroom. The hotel was surrounded by tall shady trees and
lawns. It was a heavenly retreat from the stifling and over-
powering hubbub of India outside.

Resplendent, beturbaned waiters served us at lunch.
After the last course of fresh fruit we found finger bowls
at our disposal. None of the children knew what to do
with these, so we were thankful that we were able to ini-
tiate them into the niceties of gracious living in a quiet
corner of the dining room.

The Taj Mahal as seen through the eyes of our cheerful
group of six children proved to be a remarkable experience.
We walked through the large and beautiful gateway for
our first view of the building. There we stopped to a chorus
of "oohs" and "aahs." Even my seven-year-old Belinda was
impressed by this superb piece of architecture. Its perfect
symmetry was completely pleasing, but my joyous trance
was broken when I tried to buy film for my camera. The
vendor produced a rather battered roll, for which he

wanted exactly twice the normal price. As soon as the other shop owners noticed my interest they all started yelling at me, which seemed terribly out of place, if not quite sacrilegious, in the presence of such purity of form. Feeling quite bewildered, I told them all in my most dramatic style that I didn't want any of their overpriced film.

A few minutes later, and out of range of the babble of salesmen, we walked peacefully beside the lovely long reflection pools. Hundreds of tourists from every part of Europe and Asia wandered quietly about, and one had the feeling that we were all pilgrims at a shrine of beauty.

After the initial impression had worn off, our young party took great delight in running up and down, standing on marble benches, jumping off, and pirouetting around in relaxed unconcern. This continued even when we arrived at the entrance of the Taj and had to take off our shoes to walk across the pearly smooth marble floors. There was something about the place that made the spirit feel light and gay. The high white shining domes, the glorious views of the river, and the delicate marble screens and inlay work on the walls were a joy to behold. In contrast, there was the spookiness of walking down under the ground through an incense-laden atmosphere to the tombs of Shah Jehan and his favorite wife, Mumtaz-i-Mahal.

To complete our afternoon's tour we drove to the Red Fort, where we were immediately surrounded by vendors of all types of tourist trinkets. One thin and miserable gentleman was trying to sell a useless-looking type of dagger. He decided that Peter would be easy money, and offered him a dagger for twenty rupees.* Peter had no money on him and—as I had told the children they were not to spend anything at this stage anyhow—he turned down the offer. Eventually the poor man came down to

* A rupee is worth approximately nine cents.

four rupees and you felt that if he didn't make a sale there
would be no dinner for him that night. It proved an upsetting experience for our son.

The Red Fort is a very handsome, colossal structure.
We wandered about, reading our little brochures and
looking rather aimless, until we were approached by one
of the caretakers, who offered to show us the underground
dungeons. He unlocked and opened an iron trapdoor,
through which I could see only a most uninviting black
nothingness. Our caretaker waved to us all to go through,
but we mothers were filled with strong protective instincts
and decided to stay by the door and make sure nobody
closed it while the party was down below. All the kids
went down, but after a minute Belinda returned, breathlessly saying she couldn't stand it a moment longer. The
rest of them stayed below for a quarter of an hour, which
seemed endless to us worrying mothers. Despite our fears,
the children returned full of cheer and information. They
had been shown where the prisoners had been locked up,
and where the soldiers used to shoot their arrows through
little holes in the thick walls. However, everybody, I think,
was quite pleased to be reunited in the sunshine.

When we returned to the cars, our tour guides said they
had a few more places for us to see. We went to many and
varied shops—places that had brassware, jewelry, and the
highly embroidered silkwear which is famous here. It was
quite apparent that our guides had some arrangement with
the shopkeepers, for there seemed no end to the shops we
visited. At one place we viewed the gown reputed to have
been worn by Shah Jehan's favorite wife, and we became
quite friendly with the owner. He specialized in jewels,
which we looked at with great interest. When we gathered
around a tray of unset gems, Sarah noticed a tiny garnet
and looked lovingly at it.

"How much money have you got, little girl?" the shop-keeper asked.

"None!" replied Sarah truthfully. I think the shopkeeper was so surprised to find a tourist without any money that his heart softened and he gave her the stone. Sarah's face was a picture . . . she looked as though she had just received a king's ransom.

Next morning we breakfasted hurriedly. After a pleasant talk with our host and a brief play with his three fluffy Tibetan Apso dogs we drove out of Agra toward the ancient Mogul city of Fatehpur Sikri. At the city gate we paid our entrance fee and went inside. Finding the place so big and complex, we decided to hire a guide, and found one. Unfortunately, he was not only a guide but also a monologist, one of those talkative kinds who stand for ages in front of every place of interest and deliver long harangues about points you can't possibly remember. Half-way through the tour there was a call for a toilet and we were taken to a beautiful little red sandstone room with absolutely no facilities in it, but at least it was private. I felt rather sad that such an exquisite piece of stonemasonry had to be used for this necessary but unromantic function.

The most popular event of the tour was the spectacle of a man jumping eighty feet from the battlements of a building into a large tank of water. It was a horrifying business, I thought, as the tank wasn't all that big and it was filled with green soupy water. When the man jumped it seemed ages before he hit the water, and there was a sort of ominous boom as he disappeared below the scum. However, he soon reappeared and swam to the side, where he removed his only garment, a tiny loincloth, and very carefully laid it out to dry. In fact, there was a collection of tiny loincloths laid out in the sun. Perhaps he didn't like the slimy water much either.

During the drive back to Delhi we planned to stop under some pleasant shady tree around midday and have a
picnic. We had been given parcels of sandwiches by the
hotel, and our drivers had soft drinks in an icebox in the
back of the car. At half past twelve I noticed a pleasant
area with a patch of large trees and a nice grassy verge and
suggested we stop. My driver said, "Oh, no! This is not
very good. I know of a much better place twenty minutes
ahead." All family outings are prone to this infuriating
practice and I knew what the outcome would be. After
twenty minutes no pleasant shady trees arrived, and a
little later our two drivers stopped on a dusty section of
the road lined with dirty, dilapidated houses, which were
inhabited by sad-looking people, and scrawny cattle.

"Here you are," they said firmly. "This is a nice place
for lunch."

I complained energetically. Our driver's excuse was that
they had to stop where they could buy a meal.

"Well, we've got plenty of food for you," I suggested.
But they obviously didn't like our type of food and so they
compromised by driving the cars across the road to an
Indian Oil station with a quiet and tree-lined driveway.

They left us, and we unpacked our lunches in readiness
to eat. Suddenly one of the men from the petrol station came over.

"What do you want?" he said.

"Would it be all right for us to have our lunch here in
the shade?" we asked.

"Lunch here in the shade?" repeated the man.

So I said, "Do you mind?" and he said, "Do you mind?"

So then I said, "Do you understand?" and he said, "Do
you understand?"

It became quite apparent that the poor little man didn't
understand but was trying to be friendly. After a few mo-

ments he disappeared, returning with two very nice cane chairs with the edgings covered in worn-out bicycle tires. He then went back and returned with more. I thanked him profusely for his kindness. We were comfortable now and had started to eat our lunch in peace when two stray pariah dogs appeared on the scene. These poor animals infest India in millions and they had made a terrible impression on our children. The dogs were skin and bone, with little fur on their backs. They sat and looked at us.

"Can we feed them?" inquired Susan.

"Not until we've finished eating," replied Lois.

The chicken sandwiches started to taste like blotting paper, but we carried on eating until we heard a choking sound from Susan.

"What's wrong?" said Lois.

"It's these p-p-poor dogs," Susan said, weeping. "It's so cruel to think of us eating, while they starve. I can't bear it."

We told her she had better bear it until we had finished eating. Then we gave some of the food to the poor creatures, who ate ravenously until they had consumed a whole package of sandwiches. We carried back the cane chairs to our kind host and, when our well-fed drivers returned, drove on toward Delhi.

About forty miles from our destination our car started to cough and splutter. I looked at the fuel gauge. It was registering nothing.

"Have we run out of petrol?" I said.

"Oh, no, Memsahib, just a block in the fuel pump."

We coughed and spluttered a little bit longer and finally came to a halt beside a village. Immediately all the local people came and stood around us and had a good stare. I asked our two drivers if they had found out the cause of our trouble.

"Just something mechanical. All will be well," they reassured us.

While we were waiting for all to be well, four or five snake charmers appeared with some large sleepy-looking snakes dangling from their arms and in baskets. For a few uncomfortable moments we seemed to be surrounded by them and I decided that we were absorbing the life of India a little more thoroughly than I had anticipated. I turned around at this moment and saw our driver surreptitiously filling a Coca-Cola bottle with petrol from the other car and popping it into the tank of our car.

After pouring five bottles of petrol into the tank, he announced that there would be enough fuel to get us to the next petrol station. It took the car quite a long time to start. For the next ten minutes we proceeded to Delhi in a most drunken style, coasting a lot of the time, until the car started to cough and splutter once more. To make the last few drops of petrol drain into the engine, the driver rocked the car by zigzagging all over the road, and we kept this up crazily for a mile or so until we stopped again.

"Where is the petrol station?" I said.

"Oh, very close, Memsahib."

We all got out and this time, to my relief, there was no village or snake charmers. We put another five Coke bottles of petrol into the tank and continued onward, until again we had to start zigzagging the petrol into the engine. I suggested sending the other car on to bring petrol back, but this idea didn't seem too popular. At last, with one final swing and lurch, we managed to reach a very welcome petrol station.

Safely back in Delhi, we felt rather pleased with our adventures and we devoted the rest of the day to preparing for our departure for Nepal.

CHAPTER 2

Katmandu at Last

....

Everyone was feeling a little nauseated, in the early hours next morning at Delhi's Palang Airport. We waited impatiently in the departure lounge for our plane to take off for Katmandu.

"Everything will be fine when we reach Katmandu," I told my three children firmly.

Despite our unstable stomachs, we felt much more cheerful once we boarded the Royal Nepal Airlines Fokker Friendship. Soon after takeoff a friendly steward brought breakfasts in cardboard boxes. Ann and Lynn Pearl opened their boxes and the smell of cold french fried potatoes filled the air. They both shuddered and reached for airsick bags. Poor girls! It was quite obvious now that they had picked up "Delhi Belly," as the locals so cheerfully call it.

The great river Ganges slowly unwound below us, and soon it was possible to see a low bank of cloud in the far distance, crowned with a toothlike array of minute shining Himalayan peaks.

"Just imagine," I said to my children, "in a couple of days we'll be right up there underneath those mountains."

"Look, there's Everest," yelled one of our fellow

travelers, pointing at a small mountain at least three hundred miles too far to the west. Most of the passengers rushed to the left-hand side of the plane to have a look at the famous mountain, and I didn't try to correct them. Ann and Lynn just sat limply in their chairs with their eyes tightly closed as if they were trying to mesmerize themselves into painless oblivion.

As the plane approached Nepal's southern borders, it was easy to understand why the country had remained cut off from the rest of the outside world for so long. Below us were the jumbled dark forests of the Terai, inhabited by tigers, elephants, and many other types of game. Wild rivers had carved the countryside into a terrifying and almost impassable barrier. The land rose, shrugging off its drapery of dark jungle, and gradually turned into steep winter-brown hillsides. This was the real Nepal. Only two or three thousand feet below us were the little whitewashed thatched cottages of Nepalese farmers surrounded by neat jigsaw-puzzle, terraced fields. Along the great ridges we could see paths, like trails of cotton thread, connecting the villages in this remote and mountainous land.

It seemed impossible that there could be a great city somewhere among these mountains. The tops of the ranges reached closer and closer to the aircraft, and then with astonishing abruptness the hills fell away and the wide smiling valley of Katmandu was beneath us. The valley is completely surrounded by high hills and dominated by a shimmering mass of Himalayan peaks hanging in the hazy air to the north. Nearly a million people live in this fertile oasis, which is patterned with neatly plowed fields and whitewashed houses—straight out of a fairy tale.

At the airport there were friends to meet us and, judging by the look on Ann and Lynn's faces, we needed a few friends at this moment. We were lucky enough to

be staying in the British Embassy compound and in a matter of moments we were organized into cars and started
on our way. Unlike the approach to most big cities of the
world the drive from the Katmandu Airport is a delightful
tourist trip and we were enchanted at glimpses of narrow
streets bathed in winter sunlight. Much of Katmandu
has the look of medieval times. The houses are old, and
lean almost across the street; the windows are surrounded
by intricately carved wooden frames, and life bustles along
down on the footpaths. Little shops filled with lucious
vegetables and fruit gave flashes of bright color to the
scene and our children were particularly interested in the
butcher's shop where the fat on the meat was colored a
bright saffron yellow and there was a horrible staring pig's
head, also yellow. Then we drove across farming country.
The rich greens of tidy vegetable patches blended pleasantly with the fallow rice paddies. "Toot, toot, toot,"
went the horn of the car unceasingly just to ensure that
we didn't run over anyone, but even so a child dashed suddenly from behind a building and we braked violently to
miss her. Then we had to wait for a great lumbering
Hindu cow to move herself slowly out of our path.

Our Himalayan adventures had now begun, and I felt
utterly pleased with life notwithstanding the foreknowl-
edge that never in my experience of exciting Hillary holi-
days have I not had moments when I wished I had never
left home. In fact, I have learned over the years that it's
these trying moments that tend to accentuate the joys
and beauties of a family adventure. Before the afternoon
was out, the three older Pearls had been struck down
with an unpleasant stomach infection. I congratulated
myself on all the Hillarys being hale and hearty.

Our host and hostess, Lieutenant Colonel Peter Kemiss-
Betty and his wife Jemma, already had two other house

guests, so my two little girls and I shared one room (with
Belinda on the floor on an air mattress) and Peter Hillary
shared another room down the passage with a young Army
officer. The children were very happy to go to sleep quite
early, so once they were comfortably in bed I left them in
the care of the household staff and went to an Embassy
cocktail party.

"This is the life!" I thought. "Built-in children minders,
cooks, and laundrymen. Back in New Zealand, where household help is unheard of, I would have had to organize
dinner and a minder for the children before going out to
enjoy myself.

I was wakened in the early hours of the morning when
Peter came tearing into my room and announced, "I'm
sorry, Mum, I've just been sick on the floor. I couldn't
make it to the bathroom." It was frosty and cold so I
told him to get into my bed to keep warm and went
to survey the damage. Knocking very carefully on the
door of his bedroom so as not to surprise his roommate
I waited patiently for a reply. I got no response, and when
I turned on the light I found that the young officer had
not yet returned. With the use of an assortment of large
towels I rectified Peter's accident and then we both
went back to sleep. Half an hour later I once again heard
the swift patter of footsteps and Peter rushed into my
room and on to the bathroom. For the next two hours he
vomited and had violent stomach pains. Like all mothers
I wondered sadly why it was that when children get sick
they always manage to have a different form of illness
from any that their mothers have experienced before.

I racked my brains for some way to stop Peter's vomit-
ing. Perhaps the young Army officer had returned. He had
a box marked "First Aid" beside his bed and I hoped
it might contain some type of medicine for Peter's ail-

ment. But alas, there was no response to my knocking. There was nothing for it but to wake up my host and hostess. They had almost completed packing for their return to England and had nothing but Milk of Magnesia to offer. Colonel Kemiss-Betty gallantly volunteered to go to Lois's house, from which he returned quite soon with a packet of little white pills.

We decided it would be unwise for Peter to take the pills with cold water, and of course he couldn't drink the warm water out of the tap. The complicated kerosene stove in the kitchen took quite a while to light and then at least fifteen minutes to warm half a cup of filtered water. How I wished I was back at home with my nice electric stove! Once Peter had swallowed his pill it was amazing how quickly he started to recover.

Next morning everyone looked healthy except me, and all I required was a good night's sleep. A large breakfast helped me considerably. I soon came to life and forced myself to think of the problems involved in getting ourselves into the distant mountains.

Both Ed and Max had left letters for us with a multitude of instructions and the information that we were to fly into the mountains the next day. Naturally we wanted to get there as quickly as possible, but in Nepal life moves slowly. If you can accomplish one thing in a day you are doing very well.

First we had to unearth some equipment that had been left for us in one of the Embassy houses. We finally located the equipment and it made an interesting character study. In one corner of the storeroom were four white kitbags. One was marked "Lois Pearl" and the others had the names of the three Pearl girls on them. Each had a list of contents and were beautifully packed. The Hillary equipment on the other hand was in one big brown canvas sack with a few extra oddments strewn around the place. It was all there, of course, but in rather more haphazard fashion.

Flying in a light aircraft may no longer be a great adventure for many people but we felt that the flight we were undertaking would be quite adventurous enough for us. We had to travel a hundred miles in a small twin-engined aircraft over very wild and mountainous country to the postage-stamp Lukla airstrip perched on the side of a mountain at nine thousand feet. The airstrip was only thirty miles from Mount Everest, in the heart of the Sherpa country, and close to the Tibetan border.

My husband's interest in the Sherpa people went back to 1951 when he first started climbing mountains in the Himalayan region. His experience with Sherpas on Everest in 1953 made a deep impression on him, which was reinforced by following expeditions. Ed developed a great affection and respect for the Sherpas and started thinking about ways of doing something for them in return for all their help and friendship over the years. He was able to interest the publishers of World Book Encyclopedia. With their financial assistance he built, in 1961, a school in the village of Khumjung. Since then Ed and his expeditions had built six more elementary schools in the area and supplied them with teachers and equipment. Besides this they built bridges, laid pipelines to bring fresh water to the villages, constructed the airfield we were planning to fly into; and of course had now almost completed their project of the moment—a hospital.

Foreigners in Nepal have to obtain permits before they are allowed to travel near the Tibetan border. This was our first task and we feared it mightn't be a simple one. The main government offices of Katmandu are in an old palace called the Singha Durbar, an imposing pseudo-

European structure built about a hundred years ago. Colonel Kemiss-Betty came along with us for moral support and we drove through the impressive entrance gateway and looked sadly at the remains of the elegant gardens of a bygone era. The front of the palace is set aside for special occasions, and there are great banquet rooms and ballrooms with marble floors and gleaming chandeliers.

The gracious staterooms are quite out of bounds for the lowly seeker of a trekking permit, so we hurried past the front of the building and found our way to the entrance of the Government offices. The place was a rabbit warren of tiny rooms, ill-lit and very complicated. Most of the rooms in the old days were the homes of countless concubines and it is easy to get lost when you walk alone into the building for the first time to search for some dark office. We were fortunate to have our expert guide and, with the aid of British officialdom, our permits were granted much more swiftly than we had expected.

"You are the last people to be given permits for the village of Thami," said the Department of Protocol official who had handled our case. Thami is close to the border on one of the old main trade routes through to Tibet and no more foreigners were to be allowed into the area for fear that they might cause an international incident. Lois and I thanked the official and then groped our way through the corridors and out into the blinding sunshine.

The Department of Protocol had been an intriguing place. Apart from the usual group of busy civil servants, there was a handsome young man, exquisitely dressed, sitting on a comfortable chair in the only sunny corner of the room. He did absolutely nothing except sit and look beautiful and all the workers appeared to be very overawed by him. We never discovered his official position.

The temptation to walk rather than drive back to the

Embassy was too much for us and we wandered slowly homeward enjoying the views of far-off peaks which peeped over foregrounds of jumbled sunlit houses and busy narrow streets. Katmandu can be very dusty and dirty, but it is a happy place and everywhere you walk you see smiling faces and exciting glimpses of unexpected works of art— a miniature temple tucked away in a maze of streets, an exquisitely carved window or religious figure, or perhaps a quiet little courtyard surrounded by mellow medieval houses.

Lois and I were convinced that we must procure every possible type of nutritious food to sustain our children in the high Himalayas—somewhat to the scorn of our husbands, I might say. We undertook this noble duty in the afternoon. First we bought a very large round of cheese from the "Swiss Dairy" built with New Zealand money and at present staffed with Nepali and New Zealand trained technicians. Then we filled two huge baskets with fresh fruit, vegetables, and bread. It was necessary to hire two trishaws (bicycle rickshaws) for the return journey to the Embassy and the poor drivers had a hard time of it pedaling laboriously up the last hill to the gates of the compound.

The word had traveled around Katmandu that we were flying up to the Lukla airstrip and during the evening quite a few Sherpas visited us, hoping for a ride back to their homeland. Some wanted to send a package back to their families, and it was difficult to resist their pleas. The problem was solved for us when our pilot for the next day, Ken Hart, appeared at the door with a rather sardonic look on his face. I had never met him before, but it was quite apparent who he was from his Royal Air Force uniform.

"I'm afraid there's no flight tomorrow," he said. "The

plane's unoperational. There's a screw missing in the wing
and we'll have to find something to replace it." Naturally
I agreed some repairs were desirable and he hurried off,
muttering something about getting on with the job. For
days I had been steeling my shaky nerves for this flight,
but now I didn't know whether to be sad or glad.

After a peaceful night's sleep, Peter and the two elder
Pearl girls were still looking a little pale from their recent
sickness. We now had an extra day to spend in Katmandu
and decided it would be good for the children to have a
quiet picnic somewhere in the valley. Warm sunshine and
good food would make us all better prepared for the adventures ahead. The weather in Katmandu during the
winter is particularly delightful. You can almost always
be sure of a light frost at night and a lovely sunny day to
follow. We hired a wobbly jeep, packed into it our party
of eight and our picnic lunches, and set off for the temple
of Swyambunath, only three or four miles out of the city.
As we walked up the side of the hill to the temple a group
of attractive little monkeys came trooping down to look
at us, and the children were entranced.

We entered the temple enclosure and found ourselves
in the center of a great gathering of people taking part in
an important Buddhist religious ceremony. There were
many Tibetan refugees among them, decked out in their
Sunday best. Tibetans are impressive people at any time
but when they are dressed for a ceremony they are particularly handsome and colorful. As the service progressed
we watched with interest as many of the wealthier Tibetans went up to the altar with dignity and reverence to
make their offerings. The only incongruous note was the
presence of a dozen strange, tall Europeans with long
beards and stringy hair. They wore dirty jeans and tattered
shirts or smocks, and their feet were bare. Their faces were

empty. Perhaps they were quite sincere pilgrims, but to our eyes there was something depressing and unattractive about them.

In the last few years Nepal has become one of the meccas of beatniks and other nonconformists. They come in droves to soak up Asian religion and the beauties of the area. Many of them haven't enough money to keep themselves, but they are quite prepared to beg assistance from even the impoverished Nepalis. Some come in search of drugs, which are not difficult to buy in this part of the world. A few of the beatniks are quite sincere in their beliefs, but many were abusing the generosity and hospitality of the Nepalese people and we were pleased to hear that the Government had started to make it more difficult for them to enter the country.

My youngest child refused to be caught up in these oriental splendors and kept nudging me and saying, "When are we going to have lunch?" so after a little photography we trooped down the hill to our jeep, unloaded our baskets, and hunted for a good picnic spot. We found a very attractive ridge with pleasant grass and trees. Sarah, I think, was the first person to take a sandwich. Before she had swallowed a single mouthful I heard her scream wildly and turned round to see a monkey tearing the sandwich out of her hand. The chattering creature must have jumped from a tree about twenty feet away. We had only just recovered from this when it became apparent that the entire monkey population was after our lunch. Before we managed to retreat several more of them had leaped onto the children and snatched their sandwiches away, terrifying us with fierce growls. Some of the local Tibetans, picnicking lower down the hillside, roared with laughter. For some reason they weren't being worried by the monkeys at all.

We decided to move to an open part of the ridge where there was a lovely white stupa or chorten—a rounded conical structure of Buddhist religious significance. Here we would be able to see the monkeys before they attacked. A low ledge encircled the stupa and we put our food on it. Immediately a monkey came leaping around this ledge at great speed and dropped into the middle of the Pearl luncheon. As he managed to touch just about all the food, we threw it away in disgust. We tried to frighten the monkeys by running wildly at them, but a great mob gathered beside a nearby wall, chattering excitedly and looking distinctly warlike. Outnumbered and vanquished, we retreated hastily down the hill to the jeep. No one was hungry any longer and we were dirty and dusty from our skirmish with the monkeys. To finish the meal we gave each child two tablets of Enterovioform and Lois opened a can of fizzy lemonade to help wash them down. Unfortunately the bumping of the jeep had built up pressure in the can and it exploded like a bomb and drenched Lois's dress. We all agreed that the picnic had been exciting, though hardly as restful as we had planned. During the evening one of our more cheerful Embassy friends told us that some of the monkeys were rabid and we searched our children for bites but found nothing worthy of interest.

Just before going to bed we received a short unemotional message saying that our aircraft would be "operational" next day. The expressive words "operational" and "unoperational" were new to my experience and I found them unnerving. I gained the impression that "unoperational" was constantly being used when referring to the aircraft of the Nepalese Royal Flight—mostly small STOL (short takeoff or landing) airplanes given to Nepal by other countries as a form of aid. Our plane for

the next day was to be one of these, a Scottish Aviation
Twin Pioneer (or "Twin Pin" as our English friends called
it), and it was apparently well suited to flying into a high-
altitude airfield like Lukla. I have never quite understood
how any aircraft remains in the air and my confidence
hadn't been helped by the information that out of the
original three "Twin Pins" only one was now "operational." However, Ken Hart looked reassuringly capable
and my main worry for the flight was how we were to cram
the baskets of food and equipment and the eight of us into
the aircraft.

It was a glorious morning as we made our preparations
to depart and great was the excitement among the children. Ken Hart called to see us, and in his usual dry way
said he would test fly the plane at 8:30 A.M. and if he
came back alive he would fly us to Lukla at 9 A.M. Such
talk always scares me, but I smiled cheerfully and said
we would be ready. We saw the plane being test flown
as we approached the airport, and compared to the big
jets we were used to, it seemed to be going so slowly that
I wondered if we would ever arrive at our mountain ren-
dezvous a hundred miles away.

As he taxied back, Ken gave the thumbs up signal to
say that all was well. On the ground the Twin Pioneer
was an unattractive aircraft. It was too big in all the wrong
places and had odd pieces of metal and screws hanging
loosely from various parts of the framework. Our provisions were loaded into the aircraft and securely tied down
along one side of the fuselage. Then, very collapsible-
looking canvas bench seats were assembled for us on the
other side. We tied ourselves in and waved our farewells.
There was a rumble from the engines and a great deal of
vibration as we trundled down the runway. In a moment
we were airborne.

CHAPTER 3

Into the Khumbu

....

We climbed rapidly and the little world of the Katmandu valley opened out below us. The crowded city looked strangely peaceful as the wide muddy Bhagmati river sparkled brilliantly in the early morning sunlight as it twisted its way through the city and across the fertile surrounding plains. We could see the cleft where it plunged through the mountains toward a final meeting with the mighty waters of Mother Ganges. To the north were towering mountain peaks, standing like sentinels along the Tibetan border, and to the south were miles of rolling foothills, gradually petering out into the distance.

Our plane vibrated irresistibly on over the familiar ridges and valleys that I had trekked across in the days before air transport. For some time we actually followed the main path that leads to the Everest region, and I was able to identify villages and other landmarks that reminded me of what fun we'd had on those previous trips. For some reason it made me feel a little sad. It only took twenty minutes before the vast populated hillsides, patterned with a quilting of terraced fields and pine forests, changed to a more precipitous and terrifying prospect. I could hardly bear to look out the window at this vertical

and merciless landscape with its jagged ridges and clinging rhododendrons.

We had been flying for nearly an hour when we crossed
into the tremendous chasm of the Dudh Kosi river, to
be tossed around by violent turbulence. I knew we didn't
have far to go now, for the Dudh Kosi originates in the
Everest massif and is the main river system of Sherpaland
—or the Khumbu, as it is called by the local people. We
were now hemmed in by great mountain walls and there
seemed no possible place to make a landing, but Ken Hart
waved cheerfully at us and pointed down.

Yes, there it was! A tiny brown scar on the side of a
mountain. How could we possibly land on it? All the passengers except me yelled excitedly at one another. The
brown scar became bigger and bigger until finally it took
on the shape of a rather long tennis court with a wobbly-
looking "Lukla" written in front of it.

"We'll never get down on the strip before that mountain wall comes up and hits us," I said to Lois. So to be
on the safe side I closed my eyes tightly.

"We've made it! We're down! There's Dad!" the children shrieked.

"We're alive," I thought privately to myself.

We found two excited and rather scruffy-looking fathers
waiting impatiently for us. They had both shaved off their
beards in honor of our arrival and now looked pale and
hoary after having had to wait an extra day. Neither Ed
nor Max had seen their wives or children for some months
and it was a very joyous reunion. But many of our Sherpa
friends were standing patiently beside the airfield waiting
to meet us, so the latest news from home had to wait for
a while.

There are several distinct racial groups in Nepal. The
true Nepalese are stocky and light brown in coloring and

look very similar to the people of northern India, except for a distinct Mongolian squareness in their features. They are tough mountain folk and inhabit most of Nepal, except for the northern high mountain areas. Most of them are devout Hindus, retaining much of their ancient beliefs and culture. They are a fighting people and have gained great renown as Gurkha soldiers.

In Lukla we were in quite a different world. Surrounding us were Sherpas—completely Mongolian by race and Buddhist by religion. Peaceful, cheerful, and incredibly hardy, they have drifted down from the north over the centuries and are of Tibetan origin. They owe their religious allegiance to the Dalai Lama, whose Lamaistic Buddhism is a very peaceful and colorful religion.

These two racial groups have stayed apart due to geography and the language barrier. The Nepalis speak their own national language and the Sherpas speak a dialect of Tibetan.

One of the most delightful customs of the Himalayan Buddhists is their practice of presenting katas (cotton scarves) to people they wish to honor. It is basically the same idea as giving a lei in Hawaii, but the scarf retains its freshness, if not its whiteness, and can be used over and over again. Ed's foreman, Mingma Tsering, and his wife Ang Dooli rushed forward to greet us and place white katas around our necks. Many of the other Sherpas followed suit. Feeling most important, we were conducted in triumph to the camp where we planned to spend the night.

The children ran to greet their great friend Dr. Michael Gill, a skilled mountaineer and doctor who has been with Ed on many expeditions. Mike was also the expedition movie photographer, so I brought out the tripod I had obtained in Hong Kong. To my surprise I was told

that the tripod was exactly what they wanted and that I
had been very clever. "Quite amazing," was my husband's
comment, and he little knew how true these words were.

With two and a half months of talking to catch up on,
we were kept busy that afternoon. At first we sat in the
sun and when it disappeared behind the mountains, our
Sherpas lit a big fire with a special breakwind to make
the Hillary and Pearl children extra snug and cosy. Toward dinnertime Ang Dooli offered us a large kettle of
her very best chung—Sherpa beer—which she had carried
fifteen miles down the valley in honor of our arrival.

During our meal we were joined by a delightful visitor,
Mr. Seino from Japan, who had been spending several
weeks among the Sherpas doing a series of drawings. He
added a touch of dignity and charm to our evening with
his perfect Japanese manners and tidy dress. With all the
comforts and courtly behavior that abounded it was hard
to believe that we were camping in the Himalayas. The
battered old ukulele had survived the trip from New Zealand, so now the children entertained us by playing and
singing. Their first song was "Ten Green Bottles" and this
soon became our theme song, as there were ten of us in
the Hillary and Pearl families and something was always
happening to one of us.

When it was time to go to bed my children became
aware for the first time of their friend and protector, Siku.
Siku is a back-country boy, even by Sherpa standards, but
he is extremely strong and particularly kindhearted. For
many years he has been one of my husband's faithful
helpers. Six years ago I met Siku during my first trek into
the Himalayas. He and the Pearls' special helper, Pemba
Tarkay, had decided in 1961 to leave their quiet distant
village and get employment with the Hillary expedition

carrying loads from Katmandu up into the Khumbu area. I noticed them both because of their unusual appearance. Siku wore a pair of very faded and patched green trousers left over from some mountaineering expedition; Pemba Tarkay, who at this time had no front teeth but just a gapey grin, wore very tattered Sherpa pants and a bright pink knitted singlet on his muscular body. They were a wild-looking pair and we nicknamed them the "Pirate" and "Green Pants." They reacted like children by showing off on every possible occasion and thought nothing of racing up a thousand-foot hill with eighty pounds on their backs. On other occasions they'd be full of typical Sherpa courtesy and offer to carry the Memsahibs across some mountain stream on their backs. I persuaded my husband to use them on Mount Makalu and they developed into two of the toughest and bravest high-altitude Sherpas on the expedition.

Now an older and much more experienced Siku was waiting patiently outside the children's tent. Their air mattresses had been blown up, sleeping bags stretched out, and little bags of spare clothing put tidily beside the head of each bed.

"Orr kay. Orr right," mumbled Siku, as he tenderly zipped the children into their sleeping bags. It was clear that my duties as a mother had been taken over.

Next day Siku and cook Ang Passang opened the door and popped their grinning faces into the tent. "Good morning, Burrah Sahib. Good morning, Burrah Memsahib," they greeted us and handed in a cup of tea. Over the years I have found it hard to get used to terms such as Sahib and Burrah Sahib. But they are only Indian for Sir or Big Sir or Leader. Memsahib means Madame, and even though I would have preferred to have been called

Louise I know the Sherpas like to call us by these impressive names. Normally I don't like tea when I wake up but it was so cheering to see these happy faces early in the morning that I welcomed it. "Milk and sugar?" they inquired in their best English and I replied in my limited Nepali "Chini chaina (no sugar) for me" but that Ed wanted both milk and sugar. Consternation was mirrored on their faces, for all Sherpas love very sweet tea and there was none of the unsweetened variety available. As the days went by things became better organized and a special container of "chini chaina" tea was always produced for the two Memsahibs.

Any fears we might have had about our children fading away through lack of nutritious food were soon forgotten. Our first breakfast consisted of porridge, reconstituted milk powder, fried eggs and potato chips, Katmandu bread, New Zealand butter, and Hillary honey. My children have never been hearty breakfast eaters and they astonished me with their performance. Peter had never touched an egg for breakfast in his life and I could hardly believe it when I saw him hungrily devour a couple.

"Coppee, tea, or Opal?" inquired Ang Passang, and we hastily translated for the benefit of our children. "Coppee" of course was coffee—all Sherpa and Tibetan people find it very hard to say the sound for "f". Tea was just tea, and "Opal" was Ovaltine, a nutritious chocolate drink whose name was far too difficult for the Sherpas to pronounce. Then followed a long argument concerning the number of people requiring "coppee, tea, or Opal," culminating in a few chaotic moments as the different drinks were handed round.

"Go and clean your teeth," I said to my children with a slight feeling of despair, dreading the struggle of first

finding clean mugs, then getting pure water, and finally
unearthing their brushes and toothpaste from our baggage.
Almost before I finished speaking Mingma had appeared
with three mugs of water and Siku was crawling out of
the tent waving toothbrushes and paste. Since I was sluggish because of the unaccustomed nine-thousand-foot altitude, I was very happy to relinquish this task.

I think our kind Sherpa friends thought that we sea-
level dwellers were quite helpless in our new and strange
environment and as a consequence we were treated almost
like people from another planet. The Sherpas who accompanied us on our trekking were not employed as
servants but were invited to come along as our friends,
with the exception of the cook and his helper. Even so,
I hate to think how we would have coped without their
help, for the constant travel and organization of food,
washing, mending clothes, writing diaries, and hunting
for lost belongings kept us all busy.

It had been decided that we should take the next few
days fairly easy to allow our bodies to make some adjust-
ment to the lack of oxygen at this altitude. There were
sixteen miles and a rise in altitude of four thousand feet
to be overcome before we would reach the new hospital,
so three days were allotted to this part of our adventures.
The camp was packed up in expert fashion and before
long we had left the airfield behind and were descending
a steep track down to the schoolhouse in the nearby village
of Chaunrikarka. This school was one of the seven that
Ed had built for the Sherpas since 1961. We picked out its
gleaming aluminum roof from quite a distance away but
had to follow a tortuous track among the potato and corn
fields to reach the site. Like all the schools the building
is a simple one with dry rock walls plastered with clay, a
wooden floor, glass windows brought in from Katmandu,

and a corrugated aluminum roof with modern plastic sky-lights.

The school was closed for the winter, but everything was neat and gay. The woodwork was painted a cheerful ranch-red color which seemed to fit into the mountain landscape particularly well. The low benches used by the Sherpa children as desks and the lack of any seating made our youngsters appreciate the comforts of home.

"Perhaps we should get one of the teachers to come and give you a few lessons," I suggested, but this idea was treated with the scorn it deserved.

"If you want some lunch you'd better hurry," called Ed so we said good-bye to the school and set off up the Dudh Kosi valley. Our path led across the mountainside and steeply down to the main river where the sound of rushing water overwhelmed our conversation. Down this shadowy valley little streams and puddles were still frozen hard. Pine trees clung in impossible places on the rugged slopes above us, and every so often we'd catch a glimpse of some terrific icy summit. The river narrowed as the walls of the gorge pressed in closer. We dropped down a steep trail to a rickety timber bridge with clusters of Buddhist prayer flags fluttering wildly at each end.

Earlier in the morning, we had seen prayer flags up to thirty feet high outside the houses while passing through a small village, and smaller clusters of more flags on a pass along our route. These flags have deep religious significance. They have Buddhist prayers and pictures stamped on them, which the local people believe will protect the householder and the weary traveler. They are most attractive, made of white cotton or rice paper, and add a friendly touch to the wild and lonely landscape.

A grassy spot among the rocks on the other side of the river was our lunch site. The wind was cold, so Mingma and his men built a cosy fire to warm us as we ate our bread and cheese. Ang Dooli sat some ten or fifteen yards away and it was only by pushing her bodily to the fire and pressing food into her hands that we could get her to eat. Our children were being waited on continuously and they were fast becoming thoroughly spoiled.

"Belinda, Memsahib," said Pemba Tarkay, "would you like an orange?" Belinda, Memsahib, aged seven, said yes she would like an orange. We decided things had gone too far. For the Sherpas to call our children "Sahib" and "Memsahib" was ridiculous and we told Mingma that it must stop. From then on the Sherpas called the children by their first names, to the pleasure and relief of us all. Just to show that they weren't completely spoiled, the children willingly collected firewood and packed up the food at the end of the meal.

By the time we had covered five more miles up the valley we were feeling exhausted. My legs felt like lead and I seemed to have lost most of my enthusiasm for the scenery. It was a great relief to come around a corner in the track and see our tents set up in a plowed potato field.

In everyone's life there are moments of enjoyment that are never forgotten. They are often very simple and unimportant moments, but nevertheless satisfying. As we approached the tents Ang Passang and young Nima rushed out with mugs of tea. I sat on a small rock and started to drink. The sensation of swallowing the hot liquid was quite superb—my whole body seemed to relax and be lost in the sheer physical enjoyment of it—and I noticed that all the members of the party had become very quiet, with looks of contentment spreading over their faces. Meanwhile great activity was going on among the tents, with air mattresses being inflated and sleeping bags unpacked. There seemed no end to the thoughtfulness of Siku, who handed warm slippers to each member of the family and then later retrieved our sweaty footwear.

At 4:30 P.M. the sun sank behind the western ridge and the temperature dropped abruptly below freezing. We hastily gathered around a friendly fire and kept toasting one side and then the other. The children had great fun making another fire with help from the Sherpa children in the neighboring village. Great armfuls of dried artichoke stalks were thrown onto the flames while the children danced around with glee. This was the first opportunity our children had of playing with local children and they enjoyed the experience immensely, even though the only Nepali phrase they knew was "Timro nam ke ho?" (What is your name?). But language is not important—smiles do just as well.

"Chini chaina, Memsahib!" I was told very firmly next morning as my sugarless tea was handed in to me—and I needed a cup of tea, as altitude affects my sleep and I'd had a very broken night. Ed always asked if it was a fine day. "Ramro din?" he inquired. And no matter what the day was like the Sherpas would report, "Ramro din, Burrah Sahib" (It's a good day, sir). If the weather was particularly bad they'd say, "Alikati ramro din," which means "A little good day," and we found this was a cheerful approach to life.

We weren't moving camp on this particular day, as the men were planning to carry out some improvements to a long bridge they'd built over the Dudh Kosi river in 1964. The women and children were to follow later and join them for lunch. Our tired little party didn't enjoy its walk up the valley, despite exciting glimpses of mountains and the beauty of the turbulent river. The conversation revolved around "My blisters are hurting" or "When will we get there?" and when we reached the bridge the men

were so engrossed in the herculean task of carrying
great rocks for the foundations, they hardly noticed our
presence.

We started our lunch in one of the few sunny spots,
but the wind was bitterly cold and found its way even
into the most sheltered corners. Belinda decided that half
an hour of this was quite enough for her. She climbed into
a tiny water-worn crevice in the rock and passed the time
sobbing desperately to herself. When we asked her what
was wrong she didn't know. This was all very bewildering
to our Sherpa friends, whose children are either quite
happy or very sad due to sickness or hunger. Siku and
Pemba Tarkay in particular just didn't know what to do
and looked at her very glumly. Finally Ed came along and
gave her a cuddle and she cheered up, much to everyone's
relief.

Back at camp the Sherpa farmer who owned our camping site had started to plow his field. All sorrows were
forgotten as we watched the shaggy yak pulling the simple
wooden plow and saw the man's wife walking behind and
gathering the few remaining potatoes. We were warming
ourselves around the campfire when we heard some cheerful American voices. Into camp walked Dr. Willy Un-
soeld, his wife Jolene, their four children, and two friends.
Willy was a member of the American Everest Expedition
and was famous for his ascent of the very difficult west
ridge of the mountain. He had been four years in Nepal,
initially with the Peace Corps and later with U. S. Aid.
Willy and Jolene were a remarkable pair and made of much
tougher stuff than we were. They arrived in camp carrying quite substantial loads on their backs and seemed determined to carry them as far as possible. They pitched
their tents on the other side of the field and we had a
marvelously entertaining evening together.

In the depths of the night there was an infuriated squeal from the children's tent. Next moment the three of them hurled themselves through our door.

"You careless thing, Belinda, why didn't you look where you were going?" said one of them.

"Why did you have to get up anyway?" etc. etc.

When we finally managed to make ourselves heard we discovered the cause of this commotion. Our youngest had felt the call of nature but unfortunately had tripped over a tent pole in the dark and brought the tent down on the sleeping forms of her brother and sister. Ed was just telling Peter to go back and fix the tent (he was making no move to get out of bed himself) when we heard Mingma doing the job. Mingma then gathered up the children and put them back to bed.

Our two comparatively restful days of acclimatization were now behind us and we had to face a stiff day's walk uphill to the village of Khunde at thirteen thousand feet, where the hospital had just been completed. We were out of bed very early and starting our march with only a cup of tea and a few cookies to sustain us. It was very cold indeed, but once the children's feet had thawed out and their bodies had settled into the rhythm of walking we progressed very pleasantly up the Dudh Kosi valley, over the repaired bridge, and then along to the bottom of the climb.

This was the crucial moment of our entire Himalayan holiday. If the children could manage this hill reasonably, then the month of trekking we had planned would be a success. I knew the hill of old—uncompromisingly steep without any easing of the grade. After I had labored upward for five minutes I stopped to take a photograph of the bridge almost directly below us. I put away my camera and looked around for the children. To my amazement they had left me behind by many hundreds of feet and I could hear them talking and laughing as they climbed steadily higher. I didn't catch up to them again until the party stopped for breakfast fifteen hundred feet above the river.

Feeling utterly luxurious, we stretched out in the hot sun while our Sherpa cooks built small efficient fires and prepared our food. We either sat and dreamed as we soaked up the glorious mountain views in front of us or discussed the problems of the world in a detached sort of way. It was a great joy to tuck into a large breakfast knowing perfectly well that we could safely eat as much as we liked without any fear of putting on weight. The exercise, rarefied air, and cold temperatures were a very effective slimming regimen.

Crammed full of food, we climbed lethargically up to the village of Namche Bazar. It is the Government administration center for the Khumbu and the main trading center, but I don't know any visitor who really enjoys it. There's not quite the same uncomplicated and hospitable Sherpa spirit that you get in the other villages. We had to make a couple of calls in the village—one to the police check post to have our permits examined and the other a courtesy visit to the Burrah Hakim, the Governor, of the district. The Burrah Hakim was a retired army colonel and he made us very welcome with coffee and some of the local spirit, rakshi. He also produced some candy for the children, which was a very thoughtful gesture. His staff were mostly Nepalese and all looked thoroughly bored and cold in their light city clothing. The Burrah Hakim was very smart in a well-cut suit with jodhpur-type pants and sports jacket. When each violent gust of wind whipped dust into our faces he shuddered despairingly and wrapped a long scarf around his face and neck. The Sherpas and

Tibetans sitting watching us were completely unaffected
by the cold and the wind and we could see why they
vaguely despised their masters from Katmandu valley. In
a gallant gesture the Burrah Hakim presented our whole
party with white scarves in good Sherpa tradition.

Above Namche Bazar was some of the steepest climbing of the day. With straining lungs and heavy limbs we
struggled up. Five hundred feet above the village we were
met by an old friend, Khunjo Chumbi, who had come
with his wife and two children to escort us over the final
portion of our journey. His wife's rucksack was bulging with a large bottle of rakshi and other food and drink.
Every twenty minutes we would collapse on the dry winter
pasture beside the track and be plied with tea from a
large floral Chinese thermos flask, rakshi, or some cold
fried sliced potatoes. It was an exquisite day, brilliantly
clear and pleasantly warm in the sun. Ahead of us were
golden brown fields dotted with Himalayan sheep and
great shaggy yaks. Above us thrust the fluted ice walls of
mighty Tamserku and Kangtega, both of which had been
climbed by my husband's expeditions. We wandered past
long "mani" walls—prayer walls made of flat stones with
beautiful Buddhist inscriptions carved on them—and
with great care observed the local tradition of always keeping them on our right.

Ahead of us was a fairy staircase winding between great
moss-covered erratic boulders and stunted pine trees. We
panted our way up with renewed energy, knowing our
journey was almost ended. Ahead of us, on a little pass,
was a bunch of prayer flags blowing in the wind. Far below us the Dudh Kosi gorge was lost in shadows. We
reached the crest of the pass and gazed in admiration at
the sunlit stony ramparts of Khumbila, the sacred mountain of the Sherpas. Nestling comfortably below its preci-

pices were the twin villages of Khumjung and Khunde—
and the shining new roof of our hospital. We could hear
the cheerful voices of children playing among the Sherpa
houses and the faint but clear songs of the yak herders on
the lower slopes of Khumbila. With whoops of joy we
rushed down the hill, leaping snowdrifts and icy patches,
all tiredness forgotten and our sole interest to see our
many friends again.

CHAPTER 4

A Hospital for the Sherpas

. . . .

On the outskirts of Khunde we passed a tall white chorten decorated with staring painted eyes and then climbed up through the village with its neat brown potato fields, cheerful whitewashed houses, and tall flapping prayer flags. As we neared our destination we gathered a procession of happy villagers who followed noisily behind us along the narrow stony pathways. A large welcome archway had been erected in front of the hospital in our honor and we were greeted by many more of our friends who came forward with beaming faces and placed presentation scarves around our necks. All the Sherpas who had been working on the construction of the hospital were standing in one cheerful rugged group. It would have been difficult to find a more tenderhearted but tough collection of men anywhere in the world.

The hospital was built just above the village in a sheltered and sunny position. By now the sun was making its usual hasty retreat behind the mountains, leaving us shivering in the freezing shadows. All the little houses below us had smoke drifting through the roofs as though an incendiarist had gone wild, whereas it was only the lack of chimneys which caused the smoke to escape in such haphazard fashion. Beyond the village was the low forested ridge that we had just crossed, and towering over everything were the sunlit peaks.

Dianne and John McKinnon, our resident doctor and his wife, came rushing out of their private quarters in the hospital to welcome us. The two of them were to remain at the hospital for a year, and if their enthusiastic faces were any guide, they were going to enjoy the twelve months ahead. John and Dianne were volunteers selected by our New Zealand scheme called Volunteer Service Abroad which is very similar to the American Peace Corps or English Volunteer Service Overseas. V.S.A., as we call it, had transported the McKinnons to Nepal and our general hospital funds were paying their living expenses and the modest pocket money that such volunteers receive. John would be running the hospital. Dianne was a school-teacher and would share her time between assisting in the hospital and teaching English at the Khumjung school.

Standing in the background were two bushy-bearded young men, Brian Ahern and Stuart King, the hospital carpenters. They had been preoccupied with the problem of shifting all their belongings from the cosy hospital building to a drafty tent, so as to make room for our two families. They didn't display much enthusiasm over our arrival and I can't say I blame them.

There was a general feeling that we should admire the hospital from the warmth and comfort of the kitchen. A large wood-burning stove made the room pleasantly snug, and as we entered a mug of tea was thrust into our hands. We were surprised at all the modern conveniences. There was even a stainless steel bench and two sinks which received ample supplies of hot water—if someone remembered to stoke the fire—from a hot water cylinder linked to the stove. To complete the household fittings one of the carpenters had made a large table, a couple of benches, and a comfortable bed for the cook. Sitting on the bed was a little Sherpa boy who had broken his leg several months before. His mother had been fussing over him so much that he was starting to lose the use of his good leg as well, so Dr. McKinnon had moved him into the hospital. To keep him happy and active the doctors had given him the two hospital pets—a rather mangy white Tibetan terrier and the most miserable of sandy-colored cats which had fits every week. The poor boy looked alarmed at the large crowd of people invading his retreat.

I must introduce some of the more interesting personalities among our Sherpas. Ang Pemma was the trustworthy hospital cook. His face was slightly battered and scarred from a climbing accident, but this didn't detract from his pleasant and amicable expression. Ang Tsering, one of the richest and most dignified members of the community, was working as a kitchen hand. Every time he handed me my plate of porridge I felt as though I had been spirited to the Savoy dining room in London, so serious and gracious was his handling of menial tasks. Then there was Kancha, an intelligent young Sherpa who spoke a little English and was being trained as a dispenser for the hospital. Smiling Sona, who came from Mingma's own household, was employed to do all the odd jobs that no one else wanted to do. He was a pleasant man with a fund of information on all topics, including many he knew nothing about.

One of the most lovable of all the Sherpas was Phu Dorje, a talented but terrifying type of carpenter who threw himself into his work with such vim and vigor that the building shuddered every time he struck a blow. It was never safe to be anywhere near Phu Dorje when he was wielding a hammer, but his strength and good humor completely made up for the slightly misguided use of his energy.

Tenzing Niendra was the quietest and most serious Sherpa I have met. In appearance he was immaculate, extremely handsome and very tall. As building foreman for the hospital he had proved himself a man of great capabilities. The happy and incredibly strong Ang Dawa had a considerable goiter and wasn't terribly bright, but in Khumbu, where strength is so important, this willing man filled an important place in society.

Sherpas very rarely have a family name. In fact, many are known by the day of the week on which they were born. "Ang," which is a common part of some names, is just a family nickname meaning younger or little. It is frequently retained when the Sherpa grows up.

Once we had finished our hot mugs of tea the proud hospital builders wanted to take us on a tour of their work, but first John McKinnon had another important member of his staff to present to us.

"She's probably too shy and is hiding," he said. "Yungjen! Yungjen! Come and meet the people."

Slowly and coyly, Yungjen, the eldest daughter of Kunjo Chumbi, walked out of her tiny room in one corner of the kitchen. A pretty girl with oval, serene face, she was dressed in Sherpa clothes—a long bakhu or tunic and contrasting colored blouse—but a large starched apron added a professional touch. Yungjen had trained for three years in the United Mission Hospital in Katmandu but had then forsaken the bright lights of the big city to come back home to her own family and village of Khumjung. Her English was very good indeed—an asset to the Sherpa hospital.

The main building was a long narrow structure with

an internal wooden framework surrounded by traditional Sherpa dry rock walls. Fiberglas insulation had been placed under the shining aluminum roof and the four main rooms had all been lined with plywood and painted a rather institutional cream color.

At one end were the living quarters for the doctor and his wife. Dianne is an artistic soul and she had made their room very charming with bright striped curtains, a few copper and brass Tibetan jugs and bowls, and bright Tibetan and Sherpa carpets on the floor and on the seat beside the window. But, joy of joys, in one little partitioned corner our hospital builders had installed a superb bathroom with a shower and handbasin, both with hot and cold taps. I could hardly wait for the many hot and refreshing showers that I would be having over the next few weeks. There was a little wood-burning stove in a corner glowing red and I couldn't help wishing secretly that this was where the Hillary family was going to stay.

We then paraded into the kitchen for a more detailed inspection. The room seemed warmer than ever; the Sherpas were washing our tea mugs under a steady flow of hot steamy water. As the fire in the stove appeared to be very low and the water was fast being depleted, I could see the Sherpas had not yet mastered the techniques of this new innovation and my happy dreams of luxurious showers faded away.

Beyond the kitchen was a large storeroom made neat and tidy in our honor. Pride of place was held by the food the expedition had brought from overseas, with dried milk and canned butter dominating the scene. But there was also a great deal of food of Nepalese and Indian origin, supporting the policy that wherever possible the hospital would have to live off the land.

The next large room was a combined surgery and dispensary and it looked very businesslike. In the center of the well-lit room was an efficient-looking operating table, and in one corner a shower box for the use of patients. The walls were covered with well-filled shelves of drugs and instruments, and I noticed there was even an X-ray machine and a small generator. The only thing the hospital seemed to lack was electric lighting, but everyone agreed that it was amazing what you could do with a good kerosene pressure lamp.

Feeling a little weary now, we filed into the last room, the "Intensive Care Ward" for patients who needed constant attention. We noticed its windows had been decorated with pictures of a cheerful Father Christmas surrounded by sprigs of holly. On the door hung a branch of fir tree and an attractive cluster of fir cones. Inside were three beds and a small stove that had raised the temperature to stifling proportions. "This will be the Pearls' home away from home," announced Ed.

A few yards away from the main hospital was another new building, consisting of one large central room and four small cubicles, each containing two beds. This was the "Long Stay Ward" to be used by patients who were well enough to look after themselves. It was not completely finished, as the walls had yet to be plastered with the local mixture of yak dung and mud, so freezing winds whistled around the room, making it necessary either to sit almost on top of the fire or to get into bed. In one corner of the room beside the welcoming fire was a perfectly lovely Christmas tree, decorated with painted foam plastic containers left over from the surgery. This was to be the Hillary family's temporary quarters until it was needed for patients, and we were hoping that the entire Sherpa community would keep healthy for a few days more, at least.

The raising of money for the Sherpa hospital had dominated our lives for a year and I felt very proud to see such a worthwhile result from it all. We had known for many years that there was a lot of TB among the Sherpas, that death in childbirth was commonplace, and that lack of iodine in the diet caused terrible disfiguring goiters with the more serious side effects of cretinism and deafness. Add to this the fact that five out of ten children never reached the age of twenty and you have a very great need for some well-organized medical aid. Ed had tried to persuade the New Zealand Government to back the project under the Colombo Plan* but had no success. So we decided to have a public appeal for funds in New Zealand, and the Sherpa Trust Board came into existence.

It was a worrying time for all of us. What if we received no money? Or not enough money? Or even worse, what if we lost some of the public's money?

Money started to trickle in—first a few pounds from the wife and children of a local member of Parliament, then a few precious shillings from an old pensioner. We organized a business house appeal with me making the appointments and Ed calling on the businessmen. I discovered, as others have, that many managing directors have well-trained secretaries who say their employers are "in conference" when they are really playing golf, but despite such temporary holdups the response was terrific and we collected £4500.

The turning point came when the forty Lions Clubs in the Auckland provincial district decided to back the project. They organized lectures and sold tickets. Ed, Max, and I did as many as five lectures a day and traveled thousands of miles in the process. But the Lions' support brought in handsome results—a check for over £8000.

* An international technical and financial aid scheme.

Thousands of pounds' worth of building materials, food, drugs, and equipment were donated by business concerns in New Zealand, and we received much generous help from World Book Encyclopedia and Sears, Roebuck and Company, both of Chicago, Illinois. The sale of the expedition press rights helped too, although Ed's companions claimed that he was pretty hard to live with during the couple of days it took him to write each of the eight dispatches he sent out from the field.

You will understand therefore that to see the hospital now completed after all our talking and writing and worrying was a wonderful experience.

I should hasten to add that our family trips weren't being financed out of these generous donations. We were paying for the trip ourselves. I'm sure that Max had mortgaged everything to raise the necessary funds and Ed had taken *his* normal approach:

"Well, if you and the kids are coming to the Himalayas," he said, "you'll just have to write a book about it to pay the fares."

And that's the reason I'm writing this book.

CHAPTER 5

Sherpa Hospitality

....

It was now time for us to get settled into our new quarters for the night. While our children ran from bed to bed trying to decide which of the hard wooden benches to occupy, Siku and the ever-willing Ang Dawa worked on the foot pumps of our air mattresses. I unpacked with enthusiasm, for at long last I could sort our piles of gear. It had been difficult to know how much warm clothing we would need, so I had brought a great collection of woolen garments. In the middle of my kitbag was a large and slightly squashed Christmas cake, which had been a going-away gift from my mother; next appeared half a dozen hot water bottles, a most important part of our equipment. It wasn't long before the "Long Stay Ward" became a little home away from home, and to make the place more comfortable Ed spread four bright dragon-design Sherpa rugs on the floor.

We had a large inquisitive audience of village children during the unpacking, and after we had finished I invited them to play with our children. I had brought two sets of jackstones, which the Sherpa children pounced upon, calling them "amagaga." Our daughters have always prided themselves on their skill with jackstones, but the Sherpa girls beat them easily. Much to my amazement, the little Sherpa boys concentrated on a box of plastic flowers—petals, leaves, and stems—which they put together in all manner of fanciful combinations. The boys also adored the very strong magnet that Peter had been given by his cousins in England.

Among the group in our house were Mingma's two little sons. Nine-year-old Temba was deaf, due to iodine deficiency, but he was a happy, delightful little boy, and very intelligent. He had developed a magnificent system of hand signs for conversing with people and undoubtedly was the most popular friend of our children. His brother, Ang Rita, about six years old and quite normal, was doted on by his parents. Ang Rita was fascinated with the magnet. When it was time for the children to go home the magnet disappeared with him. We were a bit sad about this but told our children that not a word must be spoken on the subject for fear of upsetting Mingma and Ang Dooli.

As this was our first night in Khunde, Mingma and Ang Dooli were having all of us for dinner. At six o'clock we donned our warmest jackets, gloves, and caps and walked down the little stony path through the village to Mingma's house. Unless you have been initiated into the method of getting into a Sherpa house, it is advisable to have an experienced companion with you. First you enter a low door into the basement of the house, where yaks and other livestock are kept. There are usually supplies of firewood and straw to trip on in the dark, and the big hairy yaks lurking in the shadows make it a creepy experience. By the light of a torch you can dimly see the steep uneven stairway leading up to the living quarters on the floor above. The stairways always have seven steps, as this number fits into the traditional design of a Sherpa house, and it's always pitch dark, even in the daytime. At the top of

the stairs you turn sharp left, walk along a little corridor,
and then suddenly find yourself in the big main living
room. It is well to remember that if you turn right at the
top of the stairs you will step into a little indoor toilet.

There was quite a large gathering of people, sixteen of
us from the hospital and many of the senior members of
the community. As time went by, many more uninvited
guests squeezed themselves into the room. This is quite
normal in Sherpa society and one of the most pleasant
aspects of life in a Sherpa village.

It was particularly appropriate that we should be spending the children's first evening at Mingma's house. Ed and
Mingma had met during an expedition to the Everest area
in 1952. At that time Mingma was only seventeen years
old but had proved himself a tough and reliable worker.
Since then Mingma had been on every one of Ed's expeditions and by sheer determination and ability had risen
from high-altitude porter to sirdar or foreman. But most
important of all, Ed and Mingma had become close
friends. Mingma is a magnificent organizer, so much so
that we always tease him by saying that he is really the boss
and that the expedition members just take their orders
from him.

As honored guests, we sat closest to the fire, while next
to us, also on benches, was a row of senior citizens. The
uninvited sat cross-legged on the floor. Ang Dooli offered
us chung—beer—and rakshi—potato spirits. Most of us
chose chung, which is a light, pleasant drink tasting slightly
like cider. Quite often Sherpa chung is served with the
fermented grain still in it, but this brew was particularly
clear and delicious. Our host and hostess offered some to
the children. Though normally we would have refused it
we felt this was a special occasion and an experience they
might never repeat, so we decided to be lenient. With

true Sherpa hospitality the children were each given a generous mugful and we warned them to have only a few sips.

It was such fun to be back in a Sherpa house once more with Sherpa friends that we talked and laughed the time away. About an hour later I was looking hopefully to see if any food was being prepared when I noticed Mingma refilling Peter's mug. With some alarm I inquired about the number of refills and was advised by Peter that this was just the fourth. We looked at the recipient of all this hospitality and decided that we had just halted the flow of beer in time. Soup was now served to us in pretty Chinese porcelain dishes, and we drank it with great enjoyment. The bowls were then collected, washed, and returned to us filled with Tibetan tukpa, noodles in a thin meat-and-onion stew. As a rather un-Tibetan side dish we were given little strips of mutton beautifully cooked in garlic. All this time our host and hostess kept trying to refill our glasses. Sherpas very rarely drink just a little. They either don't drink at all or settle down and have a really good party.

For dessert we were given fresh yak curds. It was cool and sweet and we called it Himalayan ice cream. To make it extra tasty, sugar and tsampa—ground barley meal—were passed round. The precooked barley meal had a delicious nutty flavor and we all ate huge quantities.

As our knowledge of the local language was not good, conversation was a little jerky and the children decided to bring out the ukulele and start singing. The Sherpas were delighted with this. I don't know if the chung helped or not, but we all sang very loudly and cheerfully for a couple of hours.

Then it was time for us to go home to bed, and Mingma made sure our children were properly clad for the freezing temperatures outside. We said our good nights to all the gathering, in particular to Mingma's bedridden old mother who had spent the entire evening twirling a lovely silver Buddhist prayer wheel. The lamaistic Buddhists believe that the prayers written on rice paper inside the silver wheel benefit the user every time the wheel is turned. There are many types of prayer wheels to be found in the Khumbu, ranging from the small hand ones to large, brightly decorated wooden cylinders. Some are so large that they have to be housed in a special room of a temple.

It was a clear moonlit night and the ground was frozen solid under our feet as we hurried home along the uneven paths. With one quick backward glance at the tall, ghostly peaks we ran into our house, where Siku was waiting for us with the fire well stoked and hot water bottles in all the sleeping bags. With the refinements of pajamas easily forgotten, we jumped quickly into bed in our clothes.

From this night on, Siku worked out an orderly going-to-bed program. He lit the fire, put hot water bottles in the bed, then provided a bowl of warm water for the children to wash in. Finally, after waiting around for me to make up my mind to go to bed, he presented me with a bowl of water. When I had finished he would, more often than not, wash in it himself, then empty it outside the door, where it froze immediately and formed a dangerous booby trap for any night prowlers. He would then turn out the lamp and go to his bed in one of the vacant cubicles.

I awakened at three in the morning with a violent headache and nausea, and at 6 A.M. felt so bad that I didn't dare move. "What's wrong with you?" said my well-acclimatized husband.

"I just feel terrible," I groaned.

"Well, do something about it. Get yourself a couple of aspirin."

"I can't move," I said in a lugubrious tone.

"Of course you can. All you've got to do is stretch out your hand to that ledge and you will find a bottle of aspirin and some water." He obviously didn't understand how I felt. The slightest movement, I was sure, would be the end of me as far as my poor nauseated stomach was concerned. At last, after much serious thought, I made the decision that I must find the bottle of aspirin or life would not be worth living. It was quite miraculous how within half an hour I started to feel human once more. Lois had exactly the same experience, and we were told by our knowledgeable husbands that altitude affects you more when sleeping than when you are up being active.

At breakfast that morning, most of us were quite interested to see how the younger members of our party had fared after their large consumption of chung the previous evening. None of them appeared to have suffered at all, which was quite surprising, for our sudden arrival at thirteen thousand feet was enough to have given anybody a bad headache. I looked at Lois and noticed that she was turning down fried eggs very firmly, so I assumed she was feeling a bit like me.

On my previous visits to the Himalayas I had only myself to worry about, but with three children to care for I found that cleanliness was a time-consuming chore. In the winter months in the Himalayas it is extremely dry and all the potato fields that surrounded the village of Khunde were squares of solid dust. The smoky Sherpa houses with their lack of chimneys help to add to the layer of dirt. To ensure a good start to our life in the hospital we all had a change of clothes and a complete wash. Siku and Pemba Tarkay disappeared into the kitchen with huge piles of dirty clothes and started using every last drop of hot water. They rubbed and scrubbed the clothes, with many rinses and countless cakes of soap, grinning and pounding away very merrily. With their great, tough, horny hands they wrung out the clothes mercilessly and then hung them out on lines in front of the hospital. Immediately the side away from the sun froze solid, while the other side started to dry quite quickly. Coming from a temperate land, we found this a most unusual and intriguing state of affairs, but it was no problem to Siku and Pemba Tarkay, who devoted their morning to crouching beside the lines, turning the clothes as the need arose.

With most of our domestic chores handed over to willing Sherpas, there should have been plenty of time to do many energetic and exciting things, but the altitude seemed to cast a spell over us. It was amazing how quickly a morning sped by as we sat in the sun and looked at the views and all the delightful people working at their daily tasks. At first our inactivity gave us a slightly guilty feeling, but we soon got over that and slid easily into this soothing and relaxing tempo.

As my body soaked up the winter sunlight I could see a complete little Sherpa world laid out before me—the ever-present snow peaks surrounding a snug little oasis with the twin villages of Khumjung and Khunde only half a mile apart. Here six hundred Sherpas lived their industrious lives, growing crops of potatoes, buckwheat, and a few simple vegetables. They cared for their yaks and sheep and made all their own clothing and other necessities. Now that they had a school in Khumjung and a hospital in Khunde, their material needs were just about satisfied. The Sherpas' gentle Buddhist faith shows in their democratic outlook, their cheerfulness under difficult conditions, and their amazingly high community spirit, which has made it possible for them to survive in this remote and difficult country.

Our children had no time to sit in the sun and meditate on Buddhism and the scenery, for a group of Sherpa friends came to play with them every day. Little Temba, of course, was prominent, with his cheerful smile and vigorous sign language, and our children made another great friend in Kanchi, the twelve-year-old younger daughter of Kunjo Chumbi.

By lunchtime it was so hot that you could take off your jacket and roll up the sleeves of your shirt. Dianne had been busy in the kitchen making bread and a chocolate cake, so the menu was a very popular one, with cheese and soup to round it off. "Coppee, tea, or Opal?" Ang Passang inquired.

"Bring everything!" someone suggested and the usual battle commenced to satisfy everyone's tastes.

During lunch we discussed ways and means of acclimatizing and the general opinion was in favor of plenty of exercise. With that in mind we asked Kanchi to take the women and children to Khumjung for a look at the Gompa. A Gompa combines many functions. It is a Buddhist temple containing the sacred images and the large Tibetan library of scriptures; it is a village meeting place where important matters are discussed and decisions made; and it is a community center for functions and celebrations both religious and nonreligious.

The children walked briskly across the potato fields, kicking up great clouds of dust as they went. Kanchi and Belinda decided they were good friends and, with smiles of joy on their faces, walked hand in hand together all the way. As we approached Khumjung we were met by many of the womenfolk, who clucked admiringly over our children. Belinda, aged seven, caused the greatest amaze-

ment, for she is a big child for her age, almost a giant
compared to the small Sherpa children, who develop very
slowly. But size isn't everything. At one stage we met a
little boy returning with his father from a fifty-mile trip
down valley to collect grain for the winter months. The
boy looked only ten years old, but the load on his back
weighed more than forty pounds.

We reached the Khumjung Gompa, which was looking very smart with a new corrugated aluminum roof put
on by Ed and his fellow workers only ten days before.
But now the Gompa was locked and its courtyard unin-
vitingly filled with snowdrifts. We decided instead to visit
the home of the famous Sherpa artist Kappa Kalden. His
large house has a fine location at the highest part of the
village and is distinguished by the tallest prayer flag in
the Khumbu—fifty feet high.

It was quite a hard climb up to his house and we were
all breathless when we reached the door. We stumbled
through the darkness, worked our way up the stairs, and
emerged into the sun again on a comfortable veranda. It
was a warm and pleasant spot and the artist's brilliant
son Ang Rita, aged sixteen, was sitting there surrounded
by his school books. Ang Rita's grandmother was there
too, enjoying the sun as she cut up turnips for drying and,
at the same time, rocked a wooden cradle which held
the pathetic figure of a two-year-old girl who for some
unknown reason had lost all movement in her limbs. The
tiny creature whimpered softly every time the motion of
the cradle stopped, but nothing worried the little old
grandmother, who patiently continued with her two tasks
in an unhurried, peaceful way. In this family there were
four generations living together and each member of the
family, right down to the young boy of eleven who drove
the yaks to the pasture, had an important job to do.

Ang Rita welcomed us and escorted us into the main living room, where his mother and married sister were preparing food. We received a lively welcome with much drawing in of breaths and tut-tutting, which is the Sherpa's way of showing complete admiration. Once again we found it very touching to see how thrilled the people were that we had brought our children so far to see them. Mrs. Kappa Kalden told us to go into the little chapel, where her husband was hard at work.

Kappa Kalden was sitting cross-legged in a bay window with a canvas in front of him and various religious treasures strewn about. He was so deeply engrossed that he just inclined his head in a very dignified sort of way and continued with his painting. I loved to watch him at work. His great, broad Mongolian face, with its inscrutable expression, changed rarely. Only when something really amused him would he toss back his head and roar with uninhibited laughter. A long thick pigtail stretched down his back and his old and slightly unsteady hands seemed to come to life when he held one of his fine brushes.

The household supplied seats for us all and we sat and admired the brilliant Buddhist murals that covered the walls and ceiling. In the old days, before the Chinese invasion of Tibet, Kappa Kalden had traveled over much of that country decorating the walls of many religious buildings with his magnificent traditional Tibetan paintings. We were amazed at his brightly colored and yet fine and delicate work—all of it executed with a brush. His house was still filled with piles of "luggage," which was payment in kind for his work. Bags of wool, piles of carpets, grain, and goodness knows what else were piled up against the walls of the living room. Those prosperous days had gone, but he still had enough stores set aside for a lifetime.

The children were offered curds with sugar and tsampa

and as Mrs. Kappa Kalden makes the best curds in the village it rapidly disappeared. We adults had chung pressed on us. I drank mine knowing full well that it had the highest alcoholic content in the Khumbu and that my glass would be refilled.

"Just a little, just a little," I kept repeating over and over again. But Kappa Kalden's wife just smiled. I drank some more and then she came back again to refill it. "No, no, no, please." I backed away from her in some consternation. She followed me laughing happily. This was true Sherpa hospitality. I backed away hopelessly still saying, "No, no, enough, enough," until finally I arrived at the rear wall of the little chapel. She had me cornered now, and in her excitement poured the beer not only into my glass but down my front. Not until I had drained my glass did she leave me in peace.

We had a small amount of business to attend to with Kappa Kalden. One of the expedition members had ordered a painting which had never been delivered to the hospital. After a lot of talk a little tin box was produced and carefully unlocked. Inside was a crammed jumble of papers. Every receipt and every letter that Kappa Kalden had received throughout his entire life must have been there and it was hopeless to sort any order out of this chaos.

"My father says that he has had too much to do, and will try and finish the painting in about three months' time," explained Ang Rita. It would have been useless to try to hurry the imposing old man, and as the sun had disappeared behind the mountains it was high time for us to make a hurried retreat toward the hospital. As we departed through the big living room with its piles of "luggage" and shelves of handsome glittering copper and brassware, we made our farewells. My legs felt like water after the enforced hospitality, but it had been a happy experience and a touching one, for you have to be a special guest to get such overwhelming treatment.

Peter had decided to go on ahead. It wasn't until I got back home that I realized he was unwell. It was altitude again, plus the effects of last night's chung and the two large bowls of curds eaten at Kappa Kalden's house. He was lying on his bed with a very white face and shivering with cold. I told him to get into his sleeping bag and I administered an aspirin while the faithful Siku went scurrying off in great haste to fill two hot water bottles. Dianne arrived with a book of nonsense poems which she read to Peter for nearly two hours by the light of a flickering candle. The rest, warmth, and attention soon brought Peter back to normal.

CHAPTER 6

Traders, Snow Leopards, and Temba

....

Every day we were visited by Tibetan refugee traders. These Tibetans were very concerned about the situation over the border, as this was 1966–67, a time of great upheaval in China and Tibet, with the Red Guards on the rampage. There was a tightening of control over the Tibetan people and the sacking of some of the remaining monasteries. Many of the Tibetan refugees who now lived in Nepal had fled from Tibet in 1959, when the Dalai Lama had been forced to leave his country owing to pressure from the Chinese. Many of these people had settled in the Khumbu, as they felt that here they were still near their old homeland. Now they were getting nervous about their proximity to Tibet and were selling family treasures to provide enough money to go "India side," and as far away from the Chinese as possible. Of course, when we stopped to think about it, we realized it was terribly sad that the Tibetans were being forced to sell their possessions at all, but for us it was a great sport.

Six or seven Tibetans would come to the hospital each day carrying large bundles wrapped in a faded cloth or with bulging rucksacks. They all wore their traditional clothing of a heavy woolen tunic with one sleeve off the shoulder in a dashing and piratical fashion. Their sweat-soiled mandarin-collared shirts looked handsome despite the dirt and were enhanced by ornately decorated charm cases containing Buddhist prayers worn around their necks. Their hair was long, worn in a pigtail wrapped around their heads and secured with a red ribbon. Many of them had bright turquoise earrings in their left ears. These men were mostly from the Kampa tribe of eastern Tibet. They were big, handsome men with striking Mongoloid features and fierce eyes.

They always took their time to display their goods and set them out in tantalizing fashion—silver tea dishes, magnificent silken gowns, copper and silver bowls, hunks of turquoise, and countless other objects. To add to the excitement of it every now and then a special treasure would be produced—a glorious Tibetan carpet, a silver prayer wheel, or a magnificent piece of jewelry.

For the first time in my life I was able to barter in an unhurried fashion, for we had all day and every day to reduce the prices to a realistic level. Ed and I spent about three days bargaining over a lovely silver and turquoise belt. We refused to agree to the Tibetan's inflated price. On the third day he went and sat a few yards away from the hospital with a very depressed look on his face. We felt that this was the time to act and made our last offer. He accepted and we all went away completely happy.

Each day brought something different. The carpet-maker from Namche Bazar came on one occasion bringing bright little squares suitable for covering a cushion or putting on a dining room chair. They were very charming but rather too gaudy for what I wanted. With Mingma's help we ordered six squares in less lively colors, but the children were thrilled with the original ones and pestered me to allow them to buy a square each with their pocket money. No sooner had they done this than Mingma appeared with the rest of the Namche carpetmaker's stock and presented a square to each of the six children. They were naturally delighted and the carpetmaker entered into the fun and painstakingly stitched around the edge of each gift to keep it from fraying.

The young members of the party were enjoying the traders as much as we were and spent hours each day bartering for small items with the year's pocket money they'd saved for the trip. Peter is a keen coin collector and was offered a big silver coin with Chinese lettering on it. On one side was a graceful wreath of leaves and on the other a rather fat and serious gentleman with a mustache.

"Who's the man?" asked Peter, and we were told, with great solemnity, "Shilling."

"What!" Peter said. "Shilling?"

"Yes, Shilling."

"When did Shilling live?"

"About sixty years ago."

"How much?" said the hopeful buyer.

"Twenty rupees."

"Twenty rupees? That is far too much. I'll give you five."

"Fifteen," said the wily trader.

"Six," said our son.

"Fourteen," said the trader, "that's the lowest I'll go," and that's where the discussion ended for the moment. Later Peter returned and offered ten rupees, which was accepted. Other traders soon appeared on the scene and one of them saw the newly bought coin. "How much did you give?" he asked.

"Ten rupees," was our son's proud reply. The man's roar of laughter showed that Peter had been rather badly taken.

On another day, two of our Tibetan trader friends brought some special works of art. Even before we were permitted to view them, we knew they must be extremely valuable, because they were unwrapped with such love and care. The sights that met our eyes were obviously from the gloriously rich pageantry of Tibet's feudal days. First we were shown a magnificent gold-plated crown that must have been worn by a high lama during some brilliant religious festival. It glittered in the bright mountain air, and the large clusters of precious and semiprecious stones set in rather obvious geometrical positions gave off a rich soft glow. Around the base of the crown were the remains of a magnificent diadem of pearls—most of them missing, alas. Attached to the crown were large dangling pendants that covered the ears, and there was a wide gold collar to go around the wearer's neck.

Four thousand rupees they wanted for it—far more than we could afford to pay—so we asked Mingma to explain that this crown was really only suitable for a museum.

"What else have you got?" came cries from all around and the other man opened his bundle to reveal the torn and broken fragments of a very rich gold altar edging. It was obvious that it had been torn off in great haste. What a pity we couldn't find the story behind these treasures, but the Tibetans refused to say anything, even to the Sherpas.

Western travelers know the large hairy Himalayan domestic type of cattle as the yak, but this is a vague term covering many crossbreeds of Mongolian cattle, cows, and buffalo. It is a tough animal, used to the cold hard climate of the Himalayas and Tibet. The Sherpas depend upon the yak for a large amount of the protein in their diet; they use its hide for leather, its furry hair for weaving into cloth, and its lovely bushy tail has always been treasured as a fly swat. Because of their great strength and magnificent thick coats, yaks are ideal as beasts of burden and carry heavy loads of merchandise over the high, icebound passes and along the narrow and very steep trails of the Himalayan valleys.

Behind the hospital a grass-covered ridge rose steeply for about fifteen hundred feet. This was one of the main yak grazing areas. A few weeks before, a huge white snow leopard had been observed running across this slope. That night it killed a young yak and during the next few days shifted to another area and continued its attacks on local animals.

We decided that the scene of this exciting happening would be an ideal place to visit for our next acclimatization walk and Mike Gill accompanied us with a movie camera, while Ed remained working at the hospital. We climbed breathlessly and sluggishly through the pine forest and stunted rhododendron scrub, accompanied by several Sherpa children carrying large baskets held in place by headbands. While we panted and puffed, they sang and whistled and hunted for twigs and leaves for their baskets. After half an hour we arrived at the tiny spring that is the source of Khunde's water supply. At one time all the water had to be carried from here, but in 1963 Ed and his party had laid an alkathene pipe down the mountainside to bring fresh water to the outskirts of the village.

At the spring twelve very large and woolly yaks were watering under the care of a young Sherpa girl.

"This will be a perfect shot," said Mike. "I want you to look at the water supply. Then go up to the yaks, pat one or two of them, and continue on up the track."

It all sounded very simple, but Mike had been telling us how yaks didn't seem to like him and we felt that perhaps we had come with the wrong companion. At this juncture, the Pearl family, who were accompanying us, disappeared around the rock bluff ahead.

"I'll show you how to do it," said Mike, as no one had reacted very enthusiastically to his suggestions. He walked over to the water supply. Then he advanced toward the yaks, who immediately lowered their heads and started furiously pawing the ground. Mike retired hastily, all the while explaining that it would be perfectly all right for us as it was only him the yaks disliked.

"Come on now, Sarah, you'd like to go and pat a yak."

"No, thank you," said Sarah quite firmly.

"Well, what about you, Belinda? All the Sherpas say that you're very estrong." (The Sherpas cannot say "strong.")

"No, I don't want to," said Belinda.

"Well, Peter, you're the only man in the family. How about you?"

"All right," said Peter. "I'll give it a go."

He wandered gingerly toward the yaks, but at the crucial moment his nerve failed and he kept straight on, not looking to right or left.

"Oh, well, it was quite a pretty shot anyhow," said Mike. "You go on up the hill and I'll catch you up later as I have to change a film." Very relieved to have passed the danger point, we wandered up through the grassland, and stunted bushes of juniper and azalea. Every so often we stopped to enjoy the sweeping panorama of the two villages with the deep chasm of the Dudh Kosi river below and the terrific slopes of Kangtega and Tamserku above. It was a perfect day and, apart from the lurking suspicion that there might be a snow leopard waiting for us with drooling jaws, we were very content.

Suddenly we heard a pounding of feet and a rushing through the undergrowth. Our hearts stood still with horror. Then down the mountain in uncontrolled terror came not a snow leopard but the biggest, blackest, and furriest yak I have ever seen. It disappeared into the forest below as dramatically as it had arrived, leaving some quivering humans behind. Above us the Pearls, quite unaffected by this terrifying experience and led by their indomitable father, were pounding up the slope at great speed. They seemed to be aiming for a very high, ambitious part of the ridge, and as this didn't suit me at all I decided to branch off to the left to a much lower and more readily accessible view point. We soon reached our objective, which proved to be on the edge of a tremendous precipice. The ground dropped away in one awe-inspiring leap for about three thousand feet, then continued steeply down to a wild river a few thousand feet below that. It was possible to see an entirely new valley system, with the houses of three little Sherpa villages spread out on the distant slopes like handfuls of pebbles. Beyond were row after row of peaks lining the Tibetan frontier. The view was almost too impressive for me and I persuaded the children who were sitting on the horrifying brink to move to a safer perch and look back at the bright new roof of the hospital far below us.

Our delightful friend, deaf and dumb Temba, wasn't completely stone deaf. If you shouted at him very loudly he sometimes heard, and when the doctors tried him with an earplug from a transistor radio he danced in time to the music. I had been instructed to bring a hearing aid with me from New Zealand and when the time came to try this all our children clustered around little Temba with terrific anticipation, because they all loved him. John Mc-Kinnon tried to fit in an earplug, but it was too big. He then tried a couple more of different sizes and finally one of them seemed to work quite well.

So John switched on the hearing aid, and Temba, quite suddenly, started grinning with joy. His father, with a very intense look on his face, shouted:

"Eh, Temba!"

Temba immediately turned to him.

"Oh!" he said.

"Hey! Temba! Eh! Temba," everyone started calling.

"Oh! Oh!" he replied.

Mingma was quite overwhelmed and immediately embarked on teaching his son to talk.

"You will have to be very patient, Mingma," said Max. "If we can teach Temba to talk at all, it will take at least a year for him to learn even the rudiments of speech."

It was then that Dianne offered herself as Temba's teacher.

"I've got the whole year up here and Temba and I can learn to speak Sherpa together," she said. "We'll have an hour's lesson a day, starting tomorrow."

Temba's earphone looked a little insecure, so John put a large piece of white plaster across his ear to keep everything in place.

"Oh!" said Temba. He put up his hand to feel the plaster and changed the clinical white color to a sticky gray.

CHAPTER 7

Fun at Phortse

....

The expedition still had some medical work to complete in the village of Phortse and Ed also planned to lay a water pipeline there.

The village was only a pleasant day's march from Khunde, so Max and Ed decided that the women and children must by now be fully acclimatized and ready for some more energetic traveling. Early in the morning we packed sleeping bags and toothbrushes—which I privately believed would never be used—and a few other necessities of travel. We waited impatiently for some Phortse villagers, who had promised to come and carry the loads of alkathene piping for their new water supply. Unfortunately we had sent the simple Ang Dawa to bring the men, and none of us were very surprised when they didn't come on time. Just as we were becoming thoroughly annoyed they duly appeared, led by their village strong man, a dark and aristocratic gentleman dressed in a voluminous black swinging tunic. He was given the job of shouldering a wide and ungainly load, which contained a quarter of a mile of polythene pipe.

Soon after we left Khunde and Khumjung we came to one of the most difficult and exciting pieces of terrain that we had to negotiate during the whole of our trekking. There was an enormous rock bluff about three hundred feet high and to my uninitiated gaze there didn't seem any possible way up it, or round it. The thought of Belinda wandering about on this great face sent shudders down my spine, for she walked like Johnny-Head-in-Air, even though very "estrong." While waiting for the party to catch up, I saw to my amazement the figure of the strong man of Phortse high above us. He was strolling carelessly across a narrow and exposed ledge and his awkward load looked as if it was about to tip him off the rock face and send him crashing to the valley below.

I suggested we move on before my nerves failed. The track the Sherpas had made over this rock barrier was really amazing. They had painstakingly built a narrow little ledge up a tiny crack and then constructed a magnificent staircase in the small gap between two giant slabs of rock. As long as you didn't look behind you, "There was nothing to it," as my husband so aptly put it. Everyone managed the little bit of mountaineering very well and we soon found ourselves on a wide and steep hillside with a fine level track in front of us. The next three miles passed far too quickly. I felt as though I was flying in space, for above was a sweep of brown mountain disappearing into a nothingness of vivid blue, and three thousand feet below was the Dudh Kosi river.

"Don't fall off the track, because you might roll rather a long way," I told the children, and I noticed that even the fathers thought it worth while reminding them about this.

At the end of the traverse there was a little pass on the ridge with an attractive chorten and a group of windblown prayer flags. They made a magnificent foreground for the views up the Imja valley toward Mount Everest, which was peeping over the top of the massive twenty-five-thousand-foot mountain wall joining Lhotse and Nuptse. Directly across from us on the other side of a deep ravine was the village of Phortse. It only seemed a stone's throw, but there was a long winding hill below us and then a steep pull up the other side.

The first part of the descent was through feathery fir trees and the track was covered with hardened icy snow. Mingma instructed a sturdy Sherpa to walk beside each child because a slip here could have been fatal. It was an easy place to be careless in, for the views through the pine trees across to the white peaks and blue sky were bewitching.

We reached the valley floor safely and found the temperature was almost tropical by our high-altitude standards. Yaks were grazing among shining white birch trees beside a rushing river, and we gave them a wide berth after our experiences on the snow leopard hill. We were ravenously hungry except for Sarah, who complained of a sore tummy. As she had been walking so well I explained to her that perhaps it was stiffness due to hard breathing. We ate lunch reclining comfortably on the stony ground and peeled off our winter woollies when the heat became too much for us. Then most of the adults just lay on their backs and went to sleep. Even the Sherpas succumbed to the sunshine, but they looked rather guilty about it, for they are not used to taking time off to be lazy in this way.

The children passed their time beside the river, where they found pools with thick pieces of ice floating around like huge saucers. When I woke from my pleasant rest I went down to the river and found Sarah and Susan standing on one of the ice rafts singing an improvised popular song and twisting like mad. It looked like a quick and easy method of falling into the water, but everyone was

so happy that I decided to leave them in peace. Nearby
was a little hut which housed a great stone wheel driven
by water to grind grain. I poked my nose into the little
building and could make out through the clouds of flour a
couple of the Phortse people hard at work. No wonder
Sherpa people are so tough, for not only did they have to
operate the little water mill but also carry the heavy load
of flour a thousand feet back up to the village.

The men tore themselves away from this pleasant spot
and left us to enjoy ourselves for another hour or so. But
Mingma didn't trust us alone and left Siku to act as guard
and bring us safely up to Phortse. Afternoon shadows told
us it was time to leave our picnic spot and they chased us
all the way up the hill. We arrived rather breathlessly at
the threshold of the village, which was marked by a couple
of handsome chortens and two great, long prayer walls.
Ahead of us were fifty houses set in tidy brown potato
fields.

Phortse appeared terribly lonely. The mountains
crowded closely round on three sides, as if some day they
would overwhelm the village and its inhabitants. On the
open side, to the south, the late afternoon sun sent rays
of gold onto the houses from above a deep sea of gloomy
clouds. This was the most isolated settlement I had ever
visited and to survive in such a place must be difficult
indeed. Small wonder that some of our toughest climbing
Sherpas have come from here, including Siku, Pemba
Tarkay, and Ang Dawa.

"Which house are we staying in?" I asked Siku.

"Ang Dawa's house," Siku replied.

"Which one is it?"

"Very much uphill going," was his laconic answer in a
special pidgin Nepali that he used for my benefit. This
was not good news, because suddenly everyone had become

tired. We continued up through the village and almost the entire population of women and children came to look at us. I imagine this was the first time that European children had visited Phortse. We were amazed at the number of women with large goiters and the many cretins among them. The cretins wore filthy tattered rags, but their sweet slow smiles were so reassuring that the tragedy of it all didn't really affect us at the time. They are happy people, too, for their lives are useful to the community; they fetch and carry, dig in the fields, and collect firewood. Because of this they are far better off than similar people in our so-called progressive society.

"Where is your house, Siku?" someone asked. He seemed a little cagey about it, but finally pointed vaguely over to the left where there was a cluster of houses.

"Come on now, show us, Siku," we all chorused. But he seemed very coy about it and evaded giving an answer.

We were shown Pemba Tarkay's house, which was freshly whitewashed and very neat. Much to our surprise, Ang Dawa's house was one of the biggest in the village. His parents, who had been quite wealthy people, had died leaving many debts, so Ang Dawa had a large important-looking house with very little in it except his dear little dainty wife, who was as simple and naïve as her husband.

Ang Dawa's house had come into its own a couple of months before when the four doctors of the expedition had been carrying out a very complicated program of research and treatment of the goiter that is so common in the Khumbu. They had picked Phortse and Ang Dawa's house as one of the main bases for their work, as the proportion of people affected in the village was particularly high. The main cause of this problem was the lack of iodine in the diet. Cretinism, deafness, and dumbness were extremely common and in a village like Phortse a large proportion of the people had their mental faculties a little dulled as a consequence. Ang Dawa and his wife were typical cases of this. The doctors had spent many weeks making a multitude of tests with radioactive iodine and electronic counters, X-ray machines and electrocardiographs, mundane test tubes and ghastly hypodermic needles. Treatment was by special iodine pills and by injecting iodine-bearing oil, which slowly released an adequate supply of iodine into the bloodstream for three years or more.

We quickly deposited our gear in Ang Dawa's house. It looked as though there would be plenty of room for everyone.

"What's for dinner, Memsahib?" said Ang Passang. Oh dear, here was a problem. We hadn't worried much about food for our one night's stay at Phortse. There were five packets of soup, three one-pound cans of sausages, and some rice and potatoes for fifteen of us. With such a small selection of food, Lois and I decided that the time had come for us to show Ang Passang another great culinary skill—the art of cooking fried rice.

"We won't make it yet, Ang Passang, it's too early. We'll be back at five o'clock to show you," we called as we stumbled down the dark stairs and groped our way into the sunlight.

Our children were doing handstands in front of the house before an admiring audience, but when they saw us they came rushing over to say they needed a toilet place very badly. We didn't like using the Sherpa toilets for fear of picking up dysentery and the nearest secluded spot was about four hundred feet up the mountain. By the time we returned from our successful expedition it was nearly five o'clock. There was a pleasant smell of cooking wafting down the wobbly dark stairs as we climbed into the living room.

"It's orr kay, Memsahib," said Ang Passang. "The rice is cooking."

"But you don't know how to do it," I said.

"It's orr kay, Memsahib," he repeated. "I did it." We peered into the large black cooking pot. Ang Passang had certainly done it. Instead of frying our precious rice, he had thrown about half a pound of butter, the soup packets, and all the rice and potatoes into a pot of water and was now boiling the mixture. The result was rather like a very soft and sorry type of porridge. Ang Passang and his Sherpa companions looked at Lois and me accusingly. We tried to explain that the recipe had gone a little wrong but it was useless. By the looks on the Sherpas' faces it was clear that they thought this was just another example of sea-level folk trying to cope at high altitude.

Sherpa houses don't have chimneys, but many of our more sophisticated Sherpa friends have rigged up simple methods of getting rid of the smoke or even cleverly opening a window just behind the fire so that the room doesn't become too unpleasant.

Ed had told me that on a previous visit to Ang Dawa's house he had been impressed by the lack of smoke. He also mentioned that their stay had resulted in a rather lively Sherpa party, so I didn't know how much I could rely on his judgment. Apparently one luckless member of the medical party had finished up by being put to bed very tenderly by the Sherpas.

With the abrupt departure of the sun, we all crowded into the house, trying to get as close to the fire as possible. It was not long before a heavy pall of smoke had collected in the room, two feet above the floor. It was very unpleasant stinging smoke and we all sneezed and coughed and our eyes streamed. We were crouching on the floor as low as possible and eating our thick and gooey rice porridge when we were interrupted by the arrival of some Phortse villagers carrying ominous wooden bottles of rakshi. They had welcomed the men in proper fashion a few weeks ago, and now felt they must similarly welcome their wives. In our western society small glasses of spirits are the customary thing, but in Sherpaland such refinements have not been heard of and generosity is the rule. I had just finished a large mug of water so a smiling villager reached over and refilled the mug with an equal amount of raw spirit. With a forced smile I started to sip rather gingerly. Some brews of rakshi are very much worse than others and this brew tasted like methylated spirits. When our welcomers were not looking I hastily exchanged the mug for an empty one that looked exactly the same and put it down beside me. Another jovial Phortse villager soon approached and, seeing the empty mug, splashed a whole lot of his special vintage into it. I immediately had to lift my mug, thank him, and pretend to drink a whole lot more.

Before the evening was out I had a row of four filled mugs of rakshi. In fact I had been very busy jockeying the mugs from position to position, refilling and toping up, so as to keep myself with a fairly empty mug ready for the next friendly villager to arrive.

The rakshi problem by itself would have been enough, but I was also having a rather nerve-racking time with Sarah, who announced she was going to be ill any minute. Just as a precaution I found an empty milk powder tin, into which she was eventually sick. All our Sherpa friends were terribly upset about this. They are very tenderhearted people and hated to see one of their little visitors unhappy. So they sat beside Sarah holding the tin for her as she vomited. I was so busy with the Phortse people that I paid no attention to Sarah, now that she had so many nurse-maids, and it wasn't until ten minutes later that I heard a quiet little voice saying, "Mum, come quick, I'm going to be sick again." The Sherpas fortunately grabbed the milk tin in time.

Sarah explained what had happened. "Well, Mum, the Sherpas looked so sorry for me that when one of them offered me a nice big mug of cocoa I said, 'Yes.' I drank it down and they looked so pleased. Then I began to feel sick again." I let it be known that Sarah was not to eat or drink anything more until the next day and Mingma appointed himself chief protector and sat beside her with a sad look on his face. The hospitable Phortse people then took their leave, and we hurried into our sleeping bags so that we could be below smoke level.

It wasn't a very restful night, for there must have been twenty-five people lying on the floor, very much like sardines in a tin. Every time anybody moved or tried to get outside, the entire room seemed to wake up. At 5:30 A.M. the fire was lit and as we lay in our sleeping bags we watched the pall of smoke sink lower and lower until we could see that if we didn't leap out of our sleeping bags it would engulf us completely. No one seemed in a very good mood that morning, but the blessed warm rays of the sun arrive early at Phortse village and soon we were all outside enjoying the cool fresh air.

"Can we have breakfast in front of the house, Ang Tsering?" I yelled. It seemed a shame for us all to go inside to the smoke. He leaned out of the window, a tea-towel thrown nonchalantly over his shoulder.

"Yes, orr kay, Memsahib," he said in his slow and serious voice.

A piece of plastic was spread on the dusty potato field as a table, but before our breakfast was ready some of the locals arrived with gifts of food. First to appear was a smiling matron with a large and grubby wooden cask of curds. The rather lumpy, speckled brew looked anything but hygienic so I quickly whispered to Sarah that she was not to have any. After a sleepless night it is quite difficult to consume a large bowl of very sour curds, but we gulped it down while half the village watched us. Another villager whose son had been working for the hospital appeared with a bowl of boiled potatoes, and we tackled these with a little more enthusiasm. By the time our hard-working cook arrived with fried eggs and potatoes of his own making we had lost our appetites.

There was no end to the offerings of the Phortse people, for the next person to appear on the scene brought two tiny little balls of fluff which on closer examination proved to be a couple of Tibetan mongrel puppies. They were gorgeous, and only six inches long and five inches high. One was jet black; the other, white and black. It is well known in the Khumbu that Europeans are softhearted where dogs are concerned.

"Oh, aren't they lovely?" said our six children.

"How sweet. Can we hold them?" and so on, until the dreaded question came, "Can we buy them?"

Max Pearl stood firm against a barrage of pleas from his daughters.

"Every time we get a dog," he explained, "there is some awful tragedy." But the Hillary children were unaffected by such dire warnings and as I wanted a fluffy dog just as much as they did I pleaded with Ed also.

"Of course, you can have a dog. I never said you couldn't," he told us somewhat defensively. "But don't forget, you can't take him back to New Zealand because of our agricultural laws."

"How much?" we all cried excitedly.

"Twenty-five rupees," said the owner. Our Sherpas laughed derisively, as the normal value was from five to ten rupees. The man was so old and so poor that we were quite happy to give him fifteen for the scruffy little black creature, whose fur was almost completely caked with dirt. Immediately the deal was completed, Blackie was seized by six pairs of adoring hands, and hugged and cuddled until he, at least, must have regretted the bargain.

The source of water for Phortse was six hundred yards away from the village, and for generations each household had carried its daily supply back home in a great wooden cask—no wonder the children had grubby hands and faces. Ed's pipe was going to save a tremendous amount of hard labor and the villagers were eager to help. On the previous evening a collecting tank had been built at the source and the first length of pipe had been laid. It was an invigorating walk along to the scene of activity, for the path was carved into steep rhododendron forest and we seemed to be perched high above the valley. Most of the way we were still in the shade and it was very cold. The stream and the pipe were frozen, but as the sun warmed the black plastic the ice was pushed out by the pressure of water behind and plopped down in piles on the path. It was a strange sight and the little valley echoed with children's gleeful laughter.

The men started stringing the pipe through the trees to keep it well off the ground and away from any grazing yaks. This wasn't a difficult task, but it was rather hard to keep the pipe level, so there would be a free flow of water. Mike Gill was in his element, swinging from tree to tree and getting into all the most difficult places. At the edge of the village Stuart King was building a large wooden trough, which was to be lined with a sheet of plastic and a large tarpaulin. This was the storage tank.

Working with a hundred enthusiastic villagers can be great fun, but there are problems with Sherpa hospitality. Lois and I were sitting in the sun near the water source when one of the most bouncy and handsome of the Sherpa women came hurrying along the track with a large container of rakshi. Fortunately she saw Max working on the pipeline above her and made a beeline for him. Desperate cries of "Enough, enough, I cannot drink and work" and many such hopeless remarks rang through the forest. Lois and I crept away down the track until we were safely out of range. When Max joined us later, he was looking rather pale and drawn. We comforted him with the thought that he had made a great contribution to the party by drinking all the rakshi intended for himself, the Burrah Sahib, Lois, and me.

Even though we didn't like rakshi we were most interested to visit Pemba Tarkay's home, where a brew was about to be distilled. Outside the neat, whitewashed house was a huge and terrifying Tibetan mastiff. It was tied up securely, but Pemba Tarkay was concerned that its frenzied barking might worry us, so in his usual exuberant fashion he threw himself bodily on top of the wretched creature—which certainly kept it quiet.

Inside the house a large fire was burning and mercifully there was very little smoke in the room. Everything was clean and shining, including Pemba Tarkay's cheerful handsome wife, Ang Purba. Sitting beside the window on one of the family's best carpets was an ugly and unkempt lama who had been employed to recite prayers to insure a smooth passage for the soul of a relation who had recently died. He gave us a wicked toothless grin and continued to chant the scriptures vigorously. A few moments later, however, he was pleased to stop when Ang Purba presented him with a large and delicious breakfast. First she ceremoniously placed in front of the lama a cup of salty tea on an ornate silver Tibetan stand and carefully put the silver lid on top of the cup to keep the tea warm. The lama took a sip and then very noisily and rudely blew his nose into his hand. When he thought no one was looking he hurriedly wiped his hand on the back of the carpet. Next he was given a huge girdle scone the size of a meat plate with some dabs of butter on it. He sprinkled chili and salt on this, while we watched with hungry eyes. Clearly we were not important enough to warrant such treatment.

Meanwhile the distillery process had got under way. A large copper pot of fermented potatoes and water was boiling merrily on the fire and a large container with a hole in the bottom was placed over it. To stop any steam escaping the two containers were sealed together with a mixture of flour and water. On top of this again was put another receptacle to collect the distilled liquid and finally a large flat lid covered with ice. It looked a most ungainly affair but must have been reasonably efficient, judging by the amount of rakshi that had been offered to us in the Khumbu.

It was time to leave for Khunde if we were to arrive before dark. Pemba Tarkay threw himself on his dog once more and we passed safely out into the village. As we strolled along we met Siku and his wife with their lovely little baby.

"Please show us your house, Siku," I pleaded.

"No, Memsahib," he replied. "Our house is a very poor house, not a good house." He was so ashamed of his establishment that it was no use pressing him any further.

The men had been working furiously on the pipeline and it was almost completed. A roar of excitement rose up from the villagers when the water started spurting out, first in spasmodic gulps but finally in a small but steady stream. Stuart remained behind to complete the collecting tank while the rest of us said our farewells to the headman and his council and then rushed down the hill past snow-drifts and rhododendron forest, made enchantingly beautiful by the horizontal rays of the late afternoon sun.

We crossed the river and started up the long steep hill on the other side, spurred on by approaching darkness. Our new addition, Blackie, seemed to enjoy the walk and made good time, though he zigzagged all over the place. When he nearly walked over a precipice, he was picked up by Siku, who put him inside his shirt. We started on the long traverse over the mountainside. The track was so well formed that Blackie was put down, and he rolled and bounced like a little black football for the next three miles.

Being the nervous type, I was not looking forward to returning over the great rock bluff with its very steep stairway, which this time we'd have to go *down*. There was an alternative and safer route for carrying heavy loads and taking yaks and I was hoping rather wistfully that we might be permitted to use this track.

Suddenly from up ahead I heard exasperated shouts from the children.

"We're on the yak track!"

"Who led us this way?"

"I didn't," I said. "It's got nothing to do with me."

"But you are the only person who wanted to go on the lower track," they all chorused back. I looked at Siku, whose quiet face gave nothing away, and felt sure that he had decided to give his memsahib a chance to enjoy a peaceful and safe return to Khunde hospital. In places the Sherpas had built out a great wide ledge of rocks which hung precariously above the steep and precipitous sides of the valley. Even here on the humble yak track it was necessary to remind our young folk to keep their eyes on their feet and not admire the views, as one false step would have been their last. When we puffed our way up the hill toward the hospital it was good to look back at Tamserku floating high above us in the pale light of the evening, while strange and ethereal wisps of cloud were being blown across its face from an unseen but never-ending source.

Anticipating our return to Khunde, Dianne had carefully stoked the fire and told the hospital staff they were not to use the hot water. As a result, seven of us managed to have a luxurious few moments under a warm trickle of water before it finally gave out. How much easier it was to get clean under running water than in a little basin beside the fire! The only person who wasn't clean by dinnertime was Blackie. Everyone wanted to give him a bath but we decided that he had had enough shocks for one day. Also, he was far too busy making the acquaintance of the hospital cat and dog to waste time on such refinements.

When bedtime came we didn't know what to do with Blackie. It was his first night away from his mother so we decided that someone would have to keep him in their sleeping bag. But who? Luckily, Mingma overheard our discussion and told us very firmly that Blackie was Siku's responsibility. Poor Siku's face fell a little but he gallantly took over his new job without a murmur. Next morning we all felt a little conscience-stricken when we saw Siku airing his sleeping bag rather thoroughly.

Later on in the day we had to attend to the final arrangements for three schoolboys from Khumjung school who had won scholarships to continue their education through high school level. The money for these scholarships had been donated by Senator Robert Kennedy and in very sensible fashion the schooling was to be carried out not in a foreign country or even in Katmandu but in the Nepalese hill town of Gorkha, where the new high school had an Australian missionary headmaster. As with all scholarships, parents had to be interviewed and papers signed.

Ang Rita, aged sixteen, the artist's son, was the brightest boy in the school and he had won one of the scholarships. He arrived at the Long Stay Ward with his dignified father and jovial mother heavily laden with supplies of rakshi and a great pot full of their superb curds. Then the oldest scholarship boy, Lakpa Norbu, seventeen, arrived with his mother and an offering of beer, and finally, young Mingma Norbu, a very bright and able boy of fifteen, came with his father, carrying another offering of rakshi. When the parents had agreed to all our plans for the boys they signed on the dotted line. Two of the parents were illiterate and used the age-old method of signing with their thumb print, but Kappa Kalden wrote his name in exquisite Tibetan script.

The afternoon's business was completed with the usual Sherpa hospitality. Kappa Kalden called for drinking mugs and soon Ed and I were being plied with a strong brew of rakshi by his very persuasive wife. It became apparent that our constitutions were not going to stand up to it, so we called desperately for reinforcements. "Siku," I said, "get Dr. Max and Dr. Mike. Quickly, quickly!" Not knowing what was in store for them, they came in a great hurry and were immediately propelled to a seat and forced to drink. Brian, one of the young carpenters, appeared unexpectedly at the door and he too became an unwilling recipient. Soon a mellowness came over the party and before we knew what had happened it was seven in the evening and, by the Khunde hospital schedule, time for dinner and bed.

CHAPTER 8

The Hospital Opening

. . . .

All hospitals must have an official opening and ours was no exception. At Khunde the official party couldn't sweep up to the front door in a Rolls-Royce, since the nearest road was one hundred and fifty miles away. Instead, we had been advised that our VIPs would fly from Katmandu to Khunde in two helicopters on December 18. Now that we had a definite date, the pressure of preparations increased and Ed and the other men were slapping final coats of paint on the hospital woodwork and finishing all the smaller jobs that had been left until the end. The three younger girls couldn't find anything to do so I gave each of them some big squares of white paper and told them to make labels that could be pinned on the door of each room in the hospital to explain its function. This achieved peace for the mothers for quite a few hours, and it resulted in a very bright and cheerful group of pictures, except for the one Susan drew for the surgery door. This one showed a sad-looking man lying on the operating table while blood dripped thickly from the ceiling. It was by far the most successful and imaginative picture of the day.

To add to the fever of preparations, Blackie was being a nuisance. Siku could no longer stand him as a bed companion and put him in the kitchen at night to fend for himself. Like any sensible young animal, Blackie had no intention of curling up by the stove when there was kindly Ang Pemma's bed nearby. On the morning before the hospital opening, Ang Pemma's normally smiling face looked rather lugubrious.

"What's wrong, Ang Pemma?" someone asked. "Didn't you sleep well?"

"No," he replied. "Blackie very bad dog four times—in bed," he added as a dramatic afterthought. Everyone decided that the time had come to house-train Blackie.

We worked so hard preparing for the great day of the hospital opening that most of us ran out of jobs a day in advance. None of the children had been to the village of Thami, just ten miles from the Tibetan border, so we debated whether we should take them. Many Tibetan refugees have settled in the village, which is surrounded by a wild treeless countryside, very much like the Tibetan highlands. Four years previously Ed built a school in Thami incorporating a great deal of Sherpa and Tibetan design into the building. It was painted postbox red and the effect of this splash of color on the gray, forbidding landscape was most pleasing.

The last time I visited Thami, we found ourselves in the midst of the gayest and wildest P.T.A. meeting ever held by well-meaning parents. Our reception at Thami had made quite an impression on me and I would have loved the children to see the school and meet the people, but finally we settled on a trip to Thamo, which was a few miles closer to Khunde.

Only the three eldest children decided to go, accompanied by the Pearl parents and Mike. The day was full of adventure. One of the purposes of the visit was to pay respects to a very aged and holy reincarnate lama from

Tibet. The local people called him the Thamo lama and he
lived in a little monastery above the village. The lama received his guests with great pleasure and then gave them
lunch in his private room. The meal consisted of a thin
stew made with ancient dried yak meat and noodles.
The meat had a rancid smoky flavor and the consistency
of leather. It was highly seasoned with chili. I was quite
amazed to hear that the three children ate great quantities
in their determination to show their appreciation to the old
man.

Despite their tiring walk, when the older children returned from Thamo they joined the three younger ones
in a crazy game of chasey with some of the Sherpa adults
and children. Pemba Tarkay, Siku, Sona, and Kancha
were in the thick of it. The idea seemed to be to steal
somebody's cap and then run for your life with the rest
of the gang hot on your heels.

Mingma wouldn't let us go out and dine with any of our
Sherpa friends that night.

"We must all be very strong for the hospital opening,"
he said.

"I quite agree," said Ed, remembering all the school
openings he had been subjected to over the years.

The Pearls were very happy to have a quiet evening, as
they had to move out of the Intensive Care Ward to the
Long Stay Ward, to make room for some patients who had
chosen this propitious moment to arrive at the hospital.
Two of the patients were reasonably healthy, but the
youngest patient, a boy about a year old, had badly infected buttocks and crotch. He was very sick and lay moan-
ing piteously. The doctors prescribed sunlight as the best
treatment and the first sight of his sores was enough to
make the toughest person shudder. The mother had produced two other children but they had both died from the

The children off on their adventure at the Taj Mahal. From left: Lynn and Ann Pearl, Sarah and Peter Hillary, Susan Pearl, Belinda Hillary.

After a heart-lifting flight into tiny Lukla airfield, Peter, Louise, and Sarah Hillary gratefully touch the ground.

The Sir Edmund Hillary team who built a hospital for the Sherpa people.
Back row, from left: Phudorje, Tenzing Niendra, Stuart King, Pemba Tarkay.
Front row: Brian Ahern, Hillary, Mingma Tsering, Neville Wooderson.

The completed hospital. On left, the Long Stay Ward.

Putting the roof on the main building of Khumjung hospital. In background: the peaks called Tamserku and Kangtega.

Dr. John McKinnon tries a hearing aid on the son of Mingma. The boy hears clearly for the first time.

Doctor K. Ibbertson, director of the thyroid program, examines an elderly nun with goiter.

Ang Pema, cook, in his new kitchen.

same type of infection. The complaint is mainly caused by the intense cold, which forces the Sherpa mothers to wrap their babies like little parcels. For the first two years of their lives they rarely get out of their wrappings and never seem to be allowed to kick and roll in the sun. It was quite noticeable how a Sherpa baby was muscularly underdeveloped compared to a New Zealand child of the same age, although they certainly seemed to toughen up by the time they were adults.

On the morning of December 18 we all met for breakfast looking uncomfortably tidy. Everyone was wearing special clothing that had been hidden away for the big day. Two of the Sherpas were still ironing their best outfits on the kitchen table. The floors of the hospital had been scrubbed over and over again by Dianne and Yungjen, the windows cleaned, the paths leveled, and not a thing was out of place. To complete the picture, the sun shone from a clear sky and there wasn't a breath of wind. We had told the people of the surrounding villages that the opening would be at 10:30 A.M., but we were quite ready at 8 A.M., except for Ed and Max, who were busy making hasty last-minute changes in their well-organized program for the day. There were Plan A, Plan B, and Plan C. One for bad weather, one for good weather, and another one for the non-arrival of some of our important guests from Katmandu. Nothing was left to chance.

At 9 A.M. we heard excited cries from down in the village and noticed that many of the householders were lighting containers of incense outside their windows. There was a sound of tinkling bells and a most incredible group of people appeared as if from another age. It was the dear old lama from the village of Thamo, who was really far too old to travel. His eyesight was bad and he hadn't gone on a trip like this for many years. However, he had decided the occasion warranted a visit, and he and some of his retainers and lesser monks must have risen very early in the morning to make the journey to Khunde. The lama was dressed in magnificent saffron robes and a peaked saffron cap. He was seated on a little Tibetan pony covered with rich and brightly colored Tibetan rugs, and with sweet-sounding bells hanging from its neck. Behind him came another senior lama dressed also in glittering silken finery but walking in handsome curly-toed knee-high Tibetan boots, in the bright morning sunlight. We were torn between rushing for our cameras and going politely up to the holy man to welcome him. As he approached the entrance archway to the hospital he was gently lifted off his pony and we assisted him to the hospital veranda. We asked his staff what he would like to do and if he needed refreshment, but they said they would make him comfortable in a sheltered little potato field nearby. As we gradually simmered down from this excitement Ang Rita, the artist's son, arrived with a large welcome sign which he pinned to the archway in front of the hospital.

Our next official guests arrived soon after. They were the Burrah Hakim from Namche village one thousand feet below, and various senior members of his staff and a party of policemen. We shuddered at the sight of the policemen, remembering how, some few weeks earlier, they had handled the local people very roughly at the big religious festival. To prevent a repetition of this unfortunate affair my husband had written to the Burrah Hakim, voicing his dislike of the policemen's action and hoping that it would not be repeated at the hospital opening. I am happy to say that the policemen behaved themselves quite well and, when they were needed to keep an excited Sherpa gathering from coming too close to the whirling blades of the helicopters, they exercised their duties in a very pleasant but firm way.

The Burrah Hakim looked so immaculate that it was hard to believe he had just walked up the steep hill from Namche. We all sat down and talked. I wished that I could have offered our guests a cup of tea, but according to Plan A we had to wait until all the official guests had gathered. In a few minutes the head lama from Thyangboche monastery arrived with his retinue. He is probably the most important and revered lama in this area and his monastery is the center of the religious life of the Khumbu Sherpa people. The Thyangboche Head Lama, or H. L. as we have nicknamed him, was all set for a gala day. He wasn't at all interested in any official duties and had brought his camera, which the members of an Everest expedition had donated to him. Most of the day he dashed about excitedly taking pictures just like the rest of us. I had a small present for him, a collection of flower seeds, as he is a very keen gardener, and he smiled appreciatively as he stuffed them in the front of his robe.

The Thamo lama was not having a day off. The potato field where he and his party had settled had become a scene of frantic action. The old man had been placed on a sort of throne in one corner of the field and beside him some of his monks were busily preparing various religious articles. Before the day was out six or seven hundred people must have gone before him, made their obeisance, been blessed and given a little ribbon for their neck, a small ball of tsampa, and a sip of water or chung. The queue leading to the Thamo lama was sometimes a hundred feet in length, with whole families waiting patiently for their turn. To add to the colorful scene, all the traders came with their wares and spread them out on a flat grassy field between the hospital and the Thamo lama's busy corner.

Our Katmandu visitors were due at 10:30 A.M., but at 11 A.M. there was still no sign of them. I decided that

Plan A would have to be forgotten, and I offered tea to as many of our visitors as I could. No one was at all upset about the late start to the day's proceedings, for there was the hospital to admire, the traders' wares to be searched, and a blessing to be received from the old lama.

Only one hour behind schedule, there was a thumping noise from the south and a small Bell helicopter came into view. It hovered over the village for a minute or so and then chose a large and dusty potato field for its landing place. People appeared from every direction and came running helter-skelter to watch the helicopter gingerly lower itself to the ground. Just before it made contact with the soil, its whirling blades sent up fantastic clouds of dust and the admiring crowd was sent stumbling back in wild confusion as they tried to escape from the stifling, gritty air. It was all great entertainment, and no one really minded at all. We brushed each other's dust-covered clothes and rubbed the grit from our eyes as we went forward to meet our first two visitors from Katmandu, Miss Carol C. Laise, the United States Ambassador to Nepal, and her military attaché, Colonel Jackson. We were particularly pleased to see Miss Laise as she had only just taken up her appointment as Ambassador. In fact, our hospital opening was one of her first official assignments, which seemed very adventurous to us. She had managed to combine sensible warm clothes with a very high degree of smartness and I'm sure she impressed the Sherpa people with her beautifully cut, pale blue woolen suit.

Within seconds another and larger helicopter came into view, piloted by the chief pilot of the Royal Flight of Nepal. We left our newly arrived guests standing on the track halfway up to the hospital and rushed crazily toward the big potato field once more. Again we were all forced back by an even wilder and more vicious cloud of dust. As soon as it had settled, we hurried forward. The doors opened and our New Zealand Ambassador, Mr. Jim Farrell, stepped out, closely followed by the British Ambassador, Mr. Arthur Kellas, his military attaché Colonel Gil Hickey, and finally Nepal's deputy Minister of Education.

Well, that was everybody accounted for. Tea was served once more and the children handed round freshly baked date scones made by Lois that morning, and small pieces of precious Christmas cake. For the opening ceremony the important guests were seated on the veranda of the hospital, and the rest of us grouped ourselves in front of them as best we could. The Burrah Hakim had very thoughtfully brought a loudspeaker system from Namche which proved quite invaluable with such a huge crowd of happy, chattering people.

The speechmaking was enjoyed by everyone. Ed started the function by introducing his guests and explaining that the three Ambassadors represented the three countries that had helped finance all the Hillary aid work in the area. Many in the audience had not the slightest idea what an Ambassador was, or where England, New Zealand, and America were to be found in the great wide world outside the Khumbu. Nevertheless, it all sounded frightfully impressive and added a certain dignity to the proceedings. Ed spoke in English, which was translated by Mingma into Sherpa. When he had finished, the Minister of Education gave a simple and most suitable speech which his audience listened to attentively. He spoke in Nepali and one of the head men of Khumjung, Ong Chu Lama, was his interpreter. Ong Chu is quite a character and was wearing a very dashing magenta tunic and handsome Tibetan hat. He had a most amusing method of translating the Minister's speech into Sherpa. He would listen very carefully, then take a large breath and hold the microphone very close to his mouth and talk rapidly and loudly without taking breath until he had finished a section of translation. It was not surprising that his performance met with louder applause than that of the Minister or the other speakers. As the hospital had been mainly New Zealand financed, Mr. Farrell was asked to make the final speech and declare the hospital open. He again was translated by a very nervous Mingma, who clearly didn't like translating for Ambassadors. Mr. Farrell was then led to the door of the surgery and handed a very large pair of carpet scissors with which he cut a piece of bandage that had been dyed red for the occasion.

That concluded the lay opening of the hospital and now the Thamo lama's assistant announced that the lama would like to bless the building. He proceeded to do this very thoroughly. With some sacred rice in his hand, he and the rest of the official party walked round the hospital three times while he chanted prayers and threw rice toward the foundations of the building. He then entered each room in turn, where the same treatment was repeated. It was a delightful little ceremony and we were all filled with wonder at the great energy of the old man. We were quite puffed after following him around in so many circles, but he still looked fresh and energetic when he returned to the throng of people waiting to receive his blessing.

It was well past lunchtime by now, so we sorted out the VIPs and led our guests into the kitchen, where lunch had been waiting for quite some time. It had been necessary to choose our lunch with considerable care, as our Nepalese visitors, being good Hindus, would not want to eat beef. In fact, this problem of beef eating had become quite serious in the Khumbu. It has always been illegal to kill a cow in this strongly Hindu country, but no opposition had been raised to the Sherpas killing their yaks for food. Quite suddenly the official approach was changed and the Sherpas were told that if anyone was caught killing a yak they would be imprisoned for two years. As yak meat is an important and necessary part of their diet this unrealistic approach can only cause bitter feeling between two of the cultural groups in Nepal and to my mind is a very serious matter. To overcome this problem lunch consisted of beans and tomato sauce and New Zealand pork sausages, followed by more of Lois's fine scones. All the people living at the hospital were well acclimatized and ate piles of food, but our low-altitude visitors seemed to have very delicate appetites, so we decided the occasion warranted some of our prized canned peaches and these proved popular.

Our visitors wanted to have a look at the traders and their wares before they left for Katmandu, and we walked over to admire the bright carpets and brilliant Tibetan silken robes, as well as the silver, copper, and brassware that shone so enticingly in the sun. The traders themselves were looking particularly decorative. The white peaks towered above us in a slightly superior way as though they were wondering what crazy antics we were up to this time.

No pilot enjoys flying in the Khumbu area in the late afternoon—the air becomes unstable and the shadows confusing—so it was not long before we noticed Miss Laise's pilot and Captain Jai Singh of the Royal Flight both edging down toward their aircraft. The entire gathering rushed to the big potato field to say farewell and watch the helicopters lift off the ground, and, of course, be covered with dust and dirt once more. Just before Mr. Farrell departed, he handed us a parcel from our Katmandu friends and the three Ambassadors. When the dust had settled we returned to the hospital and with great excitement opened the parcel.

"Let's hope it's bread," Lois said.

"Perhaps it might be a couple of cheeses," I said hopefully.

"Or some good onions for the stew," said one of the men hungrily. There were so many possibilities. We lifted the top off the box and quickly threw the newspaper packing aside. Underneath was a generous supply of whisky and gin. There was a stunned silence. Up here standards change, and bread and cheese become the greatest luxuries of life.

"Somebody must have given our Katmandu friends the wrong impression," said Ed, looking accusingly at Lois and me, since we had been the last to stay in Katmandu.

"Let's celebrate the hospital opening right away," said Max. That seemed the most intelligent remark so far.

During the evening Mingma organized a party for us. He asked the local Tibetan refugee minstrel to come and play his guitar in the Long Stay Ward. The minstrel was a debonair and rather sly-looking fellow, who was said to have been a wealthy landowner in the good old days. I don't know if this was true, but he now earned his living by selling a few trinkets and by making an occasional odd shady deal. His Tibetan guitar was a lovely, long, shapely instrument and he beguiled us all with his soft plaintive songs and rich accompaniment. But he didn't beguile us for long, as he was getting paid for his services. When he came to a sudden and hopeful halt, Mingma placed a jug of chung close at hand and this seemed to inspire him to further action. There were about fifty people in the room, but unless you were close to the fire it was extremely cold, so the Sherpas decided to dance. They formed a long line with arms linked and our enthusiastic children leaped up to join them. The first part of the dance was slow and easy, and I noticed that the children were looking very pleased with themselves. Then suddenly the rhythm changed. The final section of the dance was very fast, but luckily this section was short-lived and ended with a happy flourish of hissing and stamping. As soon as the Sherpas had finished the first dance all the nonparticipants joined them. This pleased our Sherpa friends immensely and we continued dancing far into the night, while the floor shook and the village reverberated to the cheerful singing.

CHAPTER 9

On the Way to Everest

. . . .

For a long time one of Ed's most cherished plans for his family had been to take them on a walk up to Everest Base Camp. He hadn't been back there since he climbed Everest in 1953, nearly fourteen years before, and he was longing to show us the mountain where so many of his adventures had started. It all sounded very familiar to us —the South Col, the Western Cwm, the icefall, and Base Camp on the drafty Khumbu glacier—and now we were to have the chance to see it for ourselves. It meant walking for three days and climbing to an altitude of seventeen thousand feet, where the temperatures would be miserably cold and the air thin and enervating.

On the morning after the hospital opening we were wakened by the usual collection of early noises. First of all, Siku broke the silence with a terrible series of coughs, each one sounding progressively closer to the grave. This coughing is a common complaint with Sherpas and is possibly due to the cold environment and the damp smoky atmosphere in their houses. Next I could hear Siku stumbling across the floor and mumbling to himself in habitual fashion, "Good, orr kay. Good, orr right," while he swept the floor ferociously for ten minutes. Then he proceeded

to light the fire and, in typical Sherpa fashion, fanned the
flames by taking long sucking breaths and then puffing the
air out in a thin, noisy jet.

Meanwhile there was plenty of activity outside. This
was the time for the herds of yaks to be driven to the high
pastures and I could hear them grunting, bellowing, and
stumbling on the stones. The yak herders were nearly always young boys and they whistled fiercely at the animals
and shouted, "Sho! Sho!" (Hurry! Hurry!) It was worth
creeping out of your warm bed to watch the yaks go by,
for they looked like creatures from hell with their big black
bodies covered with hoarfrost and great clouds of steam
puffing out of their nostrils.

Most of the households collected their water at this
early hour. From the comfort of my sleeping bag I could
hear the villagers chattering their way up to the water tank
beside the hospital. Then there was the sound of them
chipping a hole in the thick ice, the swish of water being
dipped out into large wooden containers, the grunt as
ninety-pound loads were heaved onto strong Sherpa backs,
and finally cheerful voices fading down toward the village.

I snuggled deeper into my bag, but the clinking of mugs
as Ang Passang brought our early morning cups of tea
proclaimed the dreaded fact that another day had really
started.

We put much serious thought into planning our trip to
Base Camp. It had been difficult to equip our growing
children adequately without wasting a lot of money. For
the Everest walk we managed very well by supplying them
with a couple of pairs of heavyweight jeans and warm
pajama pants as an inner lining. On top they wore the
usual shirts and sweaters, but they had two padded jackets, one lighter one in dacron for traveling and a big, bulky
down garment for really cold conditions and when sitting

around camp. Everyone had plenty of gloves and caps and woolen socks and each member of the party had two large down sleeping bags and an air mattress. I added the family hot water bags to give a touch of real home comfort. As we had to travel on the Khumbu glacier, Ed gave each child an ice axe, and he brought along a couple of nylon climbing ropes for any difficult terrain.

We planned for two meals a day, with liberal rations of chocolate to be eaten as snacks. For breakfast we had cereal plus fried eggs and potatoes; for dinner we planned a thin stew with plenty of rice, followed by custard and canned fruit, which would readily appeal to tired children. Soup, hot drinks, and cabin biscuits would round out the diet.

The packing was completed quite early so Ang Tsering invited us to dine with him in Khumjung. His family was one of the oldest and best established in the village and their house was a very large one, following the Sherpa tradition of adding on as the family grows. Most of the walls of the house were covered in rice paper with a black design stamped upon it and this gave a very sophisticated effect. There were long shelves covered with copper and brass household implements and comfortable benches with handsome Tibetan rugs for the honored guests. Ang Tsering, with his inevitable tea towel flung over his shoulder, welcomed us like a perfect maître d'hôtel and ushered us to our seats. Immediately we were served rakshi and chung in delicate porcelain dishes; cigarettes were passed around in a smart European-looking ashtray. We were terribly impressed, and the standard of hospitality kept rising. Plates of the most delicious potato chips were handed to us, and then tiny slices of liver that had been fried in butter. Never before had we been served hors d'oeuvres in a Sherpa house. This was really living. The main dinner was exciting too, for Ang Tsering had cooked Mo Mos, a Tibetan dish made of finely chopped meat and herbs wrapped in pasta and then steamed. The Mo Mos were molded into beautiful shapes and served with a type of green beet or spinach that had been pickled in a cask of salt water and chili. It was all so good that I asked Ang Tsering for the recipe to try at home.

Next morning the weather was holding magnificently for our trip to Base Camp and excitement was almost bubbling over as we walked down the hill from the hospital, waving at everyone we could see. When the last Khumjung potato field had been left behind, we plunged down the steep track that led to the deep gorge of the Dudh Kosi river. The mountains rose higher and higher above us and the delicate fir trees framed glaring white precipices as the roaring of the river rose up to meet us. In my usual careless fashion, I started to slip on the dusty path and Ang Tsering, who was puffing along behind me with a heavy load of kitchen equipment, offered me an elegant black ski stick.

"You might need this, Memsahib."

"Oh, no, Ang Tsering," I said, "I don't need it." He looked a little disappointed but made no comment. We sidled across the steep sides of the valley on a tortuous track and my eyes kept straying to the views above.

"You had better have it, Memsahib," he said firmly, and this time I thankfully agreed, for a long ski stick is perfect for walking on a steep mountain track. We crossed the river, and then stopped by a stream to have a drink and rest before the long climb to Thyangboche monastery. We had twenty porters for our tents, food and sleeping bags, and just to make things more interesting there were also two handsome white and tan yaks carrying heavy loads. They were puffing violently after the exertion of walking down the steep path and I wondered how they would fare going uphill. Nearby was a little stone shelter with a slate roof, built across the stream, and inside it was a large prayer wheel four feet high and three feet in diameter which was turned by the force of the water. It was a very charming affair but had been allowed to get into disrepair and looked rather lost and unloved.

"We'll have lunch at Thyangboche at the top of the hill," said Ed. That seemed a fine idea and the children hurried on ahead.

"Don't go too fast," we called. "It's a long steep hill and you'll get very hot and tired if you hurry."

Every now and then we could hear the children singing cheerfully far above us. We lost sight of them for some time until we came around a rather sharp bend in the track and saw Lynn sitting all alone, and looking rather distressed. In fact, much to our alarm, her face had taken on a bluish hue, and she seemed to have stopped breathing. We decided to adopt the cheerful and unconcerned approach and asked her, quite calmly, what was wrong.

Our apparent unconcern seemed to break the spell and with a long shuddering sigh she started to breathe again. She was obviously experiencing Cheyne Stoke breathing, which is very common with old people before they die and even with young and fit people at high altitude. Lynn was so upset that we decided to leave her alone with her parents while we walked another half mile up the track to where the rest of the children were waiting and wondering what had happened. Twenty minutes later we were joined by a pale-looking Lynn, who had now recovered from her frightening experience. To cheer her up Ed sang:

"Ten green bottles hanging on the wall,
    Lynn cheyne-stoked and went for a fall!"

"Whose turn will it be next?" someone said, and we continued up the hill.

Thyangboche is thought by many to be one of the most beautiful places in the world, and certainly the lovely entrance archway below the crest of the ridge, with its walls covered with bright and detailed Buddhist religious paintings, gives you a wonderful feeling of expectancy for what there is to come. When you reach the ridge, the views are overwhelming in their magnitude and quite exquisite. The monastery buildings themselves form a graceful and perfect entity on top of their little knoll; in the foreground is a pleasant pastoral scene of yaks grazing on a grassy meadow surrounded by gnarled fir trees and clumps of rhododendron; a few hundred yards away are the quaint little monastery rest house and the school; and everywhere there are mountains! Over the monastery itself looms Khumbila, the sacred mountain, with its rocky buttresses and sharp summit; near at hand are the awe-inspiring precipices of Kangtega and Amadablam; and dominating the head of the valley is the mighty wall between Lhotse and Nuptse with the summit of Everest peeping over the top.

The monks had laid bright carpets on the meadow for our comfort and we thankfully collapsed onto them. We spread out the food and had a spasmodic meal in between taking photographs and just staring at the wonders around us. The Head Lama's secretary, an old friend of ours, inquired about the plans for our return and presented gifts to our three children. Sarah received a string of Buddhist prayer beads (used the same way as Catholic beads), while Peter and Belinda were each given an old Tibetan coin. The secretary then burrowed deeply in his tunic and brought out another tiny package, which he handed to me. Inside was a bright chip of turquoise exactly the size and color I had been seeking among our traders' wares.

We wandered across the meadow feeling particularly pleased with life and soon dropped down the path into a shady forest where the snow was thick and icy. Mingma rushed backward and forward, making sure we didn't fall on this steep slippery section. The children managed very competently. We moved back into the sun again and strode beside snow-speckled fields and ice-covered streams toward the secluded nunnery of Daweche. As we drew near we heard vicious barking and saw barring our path a huge Tibetan mastiff—an appalling sight.

Mingma didn't hesitate. In one quick motion he picked a stone off the path and threw it with the skill and accuracy possessed by all Sherpas. It thudded into the dog's ribs and with an angry yelp the dog retreated farther up the path.

"Who wants to go to the nunnery?" said Mike, who planned to do some filming. I very definitely did, for it meant we could escape the mastiff for a few minutes at least. But Belinda wanted to go with her father, so they departed toward the gaping jaws of the waiting dog while I yelled at Ed in hysterical fashion that I'd never forgive him if the child got bitten. He grunted with scorn and carried on.

The visit to Daweche wasn't very successful, for as soon as the shy nuns saw Mike's camera they ran off and hid in the darkest corners. The nuns wore the same long magenta robes as the monks and they also shaved their heads, so it was almost impossible to tell male from female. After an exchange of pleasant greetings with the senior nuns we returned to the track, and I was greatly relieved to see that the mastiff had been taken to the nunnery gates and tied up.

When we passed the tiny village of Chanmitang, one of the residents came hurrying down the hillside with an old

"Teacher's Whisky" bottle filled with a powerful brew of rakshi.

"Oh, Mingma! Oh, Mingma!" the man said. It was clear that we would have to stop and be sociable. From the folds of his tunic he brought out the usual delicate little porcelain dish and rubbed it carefully on a flap of his clothing, filled it, and offered it to me to drink. I will never get used to this "on the march" hospitality, for I find half a cup of raw spirit on an empty stomach is most damaging to the system, especially when you are puffing your way up a Himalayan mountainside. One of Ed's expedition members had called rakshi "Helicopter Juice," because, after drinking it, he always felt like a lost helicopter beating its way breathlessly across the countryside.

"Do I have to drink it all?" I said to Mingma.

"No," was the very definite reply, so, thankfully, I took one minute sip and returned the cup. Mingma didn't escape so easily. He took a few tentative sips and handed back the cup, but it was pushed into his hands over and over again, until, finally, shrugging his shoulders, he drank two little dishes of the liquor.

As we continued our walk, memories of a previous visit to Chanmitang came flooding back. I had been searching for some Tibetan Apso puppies and was directed to one of the bigger houses of the village. In normal Sherpa fashion I wandered unheralded into the main room, where I found a celebration going on. There were many people in the house and much drinking of chung, rakshi, and tea. At one end of the room an impressive elderly Buddhist priest was chanting prayers, every now and then stopping to ring a bell. Near him was a long bumpy something covered in a rug. I suddenly saw with horror and embarrassment that I had walked in on a funeral. My first thought was to get out as quickly as possible, but after I had calmed down a little, I realized that the people present were only too happy to have me with them. Death is not such a final thing for the Sherpas, with their belief in reincarnation, and even the old man whose wife had just died was talking and smiling quite happily to his neighbors. In fact, I think I added a pleasant diversion, and ended up by buying a couple of puppies for twelve rupees each.

Soon we came to another bridge, where the wild torrent of the Imja river crashed through a deep narrow chasm over ice-encrusted rocks. It was an awe-inspiring place and, if you had the nerve to take your eyes off the bridge for a moment, there was a glorious view of the steep and shapely peak of Amadablam.

The next portion of our journey was very much uphill. Ed stayed behind to give me a helpful push now and then. The track wound along the steep sides above the river and was quite exposed. This is the route the Sherpas believe the great Buddhist teacher, the Guru Rimpoche, took when he left India to bring the Buddhist faith to the people of Tibet. Alongside the path was an overhanging rock where the local people say the guru sheltered for the night, and farther on was a large flat stone with an imprint of his foot. There were many chortens and prayer walls on this historic portion of our path; many times we would have to branch off to the left so as to pass these on the correct side. At one stage, I saw a huge white-faced yak coming down the track toward me and decided not to carry local customs to extremes. When I rounded the chorten on the wrong side I found that the yak had decided to be careful too and had gone off up the mountainside to lurk behind a large juniper bush.

By four o'clock we had all arrived at the remote mountain village of Pangboche, a cold and drafty spot. Ang Nima, one of Mingma's friends, offered us his house for the night, but there were so many of us that we decided to pitch our tents in the potato field out front. We used the house's warm living room for meals.

When traveling with light rations, as we were on this occasion, we followed the rule that the Sherpas and Sahibs kept fairly well to their own food, apart from such things as milk powder, sugar, dried soups, and meat. We had tried cooking the same meals, but the Sherpas didn't like our underspiced food, and Mingma very definitely disapproved of his men eating our precious stores. "Sherpa khana very good for Sherpas but not so good for New Zealand people," he explained to our worried children. After our own dinner, we watched the Sherpas preparing their food. It was one of the most unappetizing meals you could imagine, consisting of a gluey mess of mashed potatoes and buckwheat flour. They ate this with their fingers and flavored it with strong chili and salt. I decided that we would find it pretty difficult to live on this sort of "khana."

It was bitterly cold when we stumbled out of bed next day. The sun hadn't yet reached the camp. Our footwear was cold and unyielding, and there were a number of complaints from the members of the expedition who were not used to having frozen boots. After a hurried cup of tea and a couple of biscuits, we walked as fast as our breath would allow up the winding valley track toward the sun, which was now lighting the mountain tops. The path was a sheet of ice, as most of it seemed to be the bed of a stream. It was so cold that no matter how hard and how fast we went, we couldn't warm up, and the sunlit slopes kept tantalizingly beyond our reach. We came to a dark and wind-swept valley that felt like a frozen chamber of horrors. The temperature dropped even lower. I noticed that Belinda was quietly sobbing to herself with misery. We decided this wasn't a very good way of enjoying our trip to Base Camp, so we stopped and rubbed the children's hands and feet and gave them some chocolate to raise their body temperatures and their morale.

We struggled up a steep ridge, leaving the path far behind, and every step seemed a violent effort even though we were only at an altitude of fourteen thousand feet. I wondered how I would ever make it to higher altitudes. We reached the top of the ridge and all our struggles were forgotten, for the most unexpected view lay ahead. I felt as though I had suddenly come to another land or even another planet. The narrow valleys with trees clinging to their sides had been left behind and in front of us was a broad valley edged by huge precipitous peaks that seemed to be leaning inward, they were so steep. The vegetation of the flat valley floor was frozen a golden brown and a shining ice stream ran down the center of it. Several small summer yak grazing villages looked lonely and uninhabited amid the vastness of this great hidden valley, and the small fields around the houses looked no bigger than postage stamps. There must have been thousands of acres of summer pasture and the air was so clear that even the dullest stone seemed to shine. The sky was such a deep blue that you felt as if you were looking far out into space into a sort of inky endless haze. We ran with joyous abandon down the scrub-covered slopes toward the summer village of Pheriche, and on the way we stopped to gather branches of juniper bush to use as firewood. At the deserted village, the Sherpas had already started a fire to cook our breakfasts. We peered into the empty little stone cottages, many of them with sprouting sod roofs, and explored the frozen stream which was edged with stunted bushes decked in brilliant autumn coloring.

"You had better clean your teeth," I said, and the children found it a novel idea to stand on a sheet of ice and perform their daily ablutions. When our meal was prepared, we sat cosily in the shelter of a stone wall and ate a vast amount of porridge, eggs, and potatoes. The others seemed to enjoy the food but it sat rather heavily on my stomach and I resolved in future to eat very carefully and lightly.

The apparent flatness of the valley was a little misleading, for we found ourselves puffing breathlessly as we traveled along. We made many excuses for rests and Siku always had a water bottle handy, for with our rapid breathing we were becoming very dehydrated. To our left Taweche and Chobutse became more towering and impressive than ever and Mike and Ed worked out a dozen imaginary routes up their impossible ridges. At the second summer village we fell in love with a tiny cottage and vowed that sometime we'd spend a night there. Its roof was covered in sods topped with brilliant-colored autumn grass and its little courtyard was pleasantly warm and cosy for tired travelers. Sadly we hurried on toward a drastic-looking hillside that must once have been the terminal face of the giant Khumbu glacier. It looked at least five hundred feet high and it proved a long hard drag for our unacclimatized bodies. Near the top, the thundering waters of the Khumbu river barred our way, bridged only by an insecure layer of ice and snow. Crossing it looked hazardous indeed, but the indefatigable Mingma took us safely over. On the other side were two little stone houses surrounded by more golden grass. We stretched out luxuriously on the soft ground and soon felt refreshed. I was continuously being amazed by the amount of beautiful grassland that appeared in every direction as we climbed higher. "This is where the Thyangboche people bring their yaks," Mingma said. It seemed a suitably inspiring place for the monks to spend some of their time.

The hill above us was even steeper, and halfway up it we had to stop for Belinda. An argument with her sister—which at home would have meant nothing—had resulted in much sad weeping. At high altitudes everyone tends to be more emotional, and when you are having to breathe and weep very hard at the same time it is almost impossible to do both successfully. Soon she was gulping wildly for breath and we rushed to comfort her and jolly her out of her sadness by suggesting various medications in the form of hot tea, a bar of chocolate, a biscuit, or just a swig of water. It wasn't long before all this good treatment brought results, and we carried on.

On the crest of the hill a line of prayer flags waved maddeningly at us for a very long time. The thought of the view of Everest from the summit was the only incentive that forced me up the last slope. But to my disappointment the terminal face of the Khumbu glacier blocked out everything. We sidled carefully around this huge, shining mass of ice until at last we could see the whole valley. It was a sparkling scene of loneliness and immensity. Everest was still hiding like a slumbering giant behind the icy buttresses of Nuptse and it was Pumori, a lovely, graceful snow peak to the left, that was the focal point.

The lateral moraine trough beside the glacier was surprisingly wide and there was still quite a lot of vegetation. The main obstacle seemed to be the almost continuous sheets of ice from frozen streams and Mingma instructed the Sherpas to keep a close eye on the children. On the widest and most glassy section, Phu Dorje swung Belinda onto his shoulders and galloped off, gamboling over the ice as if it were a sandy beach.

"It's easy going now," Ed called to the stragglers which

included me. "We'll be at Lobuje in no time. Then we can camp." Despite these encouraging words we found ourselves puffing and laboring up the easy valley as if it were a steep mountain slope. But our mood was one of lively good cheer, for the sparkling beauty of the scenery outweighed every hardship. The camp site at last appeared and it looked the most beautiful place that I had ever had the luck to camp in. Soon the two exhausted yaks had been relieved of their loads and were having their first good food of the day while the bells round their necks jingled merrily. After half an hour of intense munching, they tossed their heads, waved their amusing tufted tails, and galloped skittishly about like overgrown puppies. A comfortable camp was quickly established with plenty of good sleeping accommodation for our porters and Sherpas in a little stone house. There was a frozen pond nearby where the children skated dangerously in soft-soled slippers. The adults busied themselves with preparations for the evening.

"Now this should be really cosy," Ed said. "We'll turn our big tent into a sort of mess tent. There'll be such a fug inside that you'll find it hard to believe that you're at fifteen thousand, five hundred feet."

We all agreed this would be a fine idea, as the smoke billowing out of the door of the stone hut was definitely going to be too much for our eyes and lungs. Ed had brought two little kerosene burners, which he now filled very carefully and set up in the middle of our tent.

"When the sun goes down," he continued, "we'll light them and then everybody can come and sit down on air mattresses and be perfectly comfortable."

Almost within seconds the sun vanished behind the mountains and we found ourselves shivering in deep-freeze conditions. We were amazed at the difference in temperature between our camp at Pangboche and our present camp. The children were still cavorting on the ice, completely oblivious to all discomfort.

"Hurry up inside before you freeze to death," I called, but it was some time before they took any notice.

Ed soon had the two little burners blazing busily, though rather a lot of yellow flame was spurting from them.

"It'll die down soon," said Ed. "They have to get heated up."

I went outside the tent to struggle into my thickest clothing and when I returned one of the burners had started to splutter.

"I'll fix that," said Ed. "You all go and sit down and relax." And he disappeared outside.

We zipped up the tent door, ready for the promised fug, but with only one burner in action it didn't happen. Ed poked his head in to say that the sputtering burner was definitely not working, so we would have to make do with just the one. He sat down beside me with an infuriatingly cheerful look on his face and we all pretended it was great fun.

Suddenly Lois let out a wail. "I'm frozen to the tent wall!"

"My eyes are stinging from the fumes of that wretched burner," I chorused.

"What nonsense," the men said, "everything is fine." But, goaded by one another, Lois and I felt sufficiently brave to tell the men exactly what we thought about our present environment.

"It's freezing."

"We've all got headaches."

"It's uncomfortable sitting cross-legged on the ground and if this is the way Himalayan heroes live, we think you're all mad, unfeeling monsters!"

At this crucial moment Siku opened the tent door and passed in four full hot water bottles. We quickly slipped them into the sleeping bags before they turned to ice, hoping that the men hadn't noticed. The last remaining burner, obviously not designed for high altitudes, was filling the tent with fumes, so we had to put it outside, as well, leaving us with nothing but body warmth to heat the tent.

"Let's play a game," someone sensibly suggested, and we ended up by playing the memory game. "I went to the store and bought some soap, coffee, and dried figs, etc., etc.," ad infinitum. Funnily enough the time passed quickly and I don't think anyone was particularly cold. At half past five, dinner appeared and was quickly eaten. By six o'clock we had finished the meal and were wondering what to do next.

"Under these conditions you just go to bed," was the verdict of the experienced Himalayan travelers.

"What?" I said in disbelief. "It's only six o'clock and we won't be getting up until seven next morning. That's thirteen hours lying in my sleeping bag."

"Well, stay up if you like," I was told, "but you won't be very comfortable." Lois and I looked at one another in amazement. So this was the way these high-altitude mountain climbers lived!

"Do you mean to say, that for night after night you crawl into your sleeping bags as soon as you have finished climbing, even in the middle of the afternoon, and just stay there uncomfortable and cold, eating sloppy uncooked food and not being able to sleep because of the altitude?" I inquired.

"It doesn't even sound human," said Lois.

"We live perfectly comfortably," said Ed in tones as freezing as the temperature outside.

And I suppose it was possible, after a fashion, as long as they were tough enough to put up with such endless discomforts while feeling debilitated and utterly miserable. I was realizing that books give a rather false impression of what it's like on an expedition. You read mostly about the dramatic moments and the glorious panoramas in an understated sort of way and there isn't much about the uncomfortable facts of day-to-day living. We had already found that most of us were more emotional above fourteen thousand feet, and it was becoming more and more of an effort to think and execute our thoughts in an efficient way. The intense cold and the altitude made us tired and climbing a small hill at fifteen thousand feet had become a mental and physical nightmare. Headaches had become part of the daily routine and all members of our party at Lobuje were dosing themselves with aspirin. Food had lost its interest for most of us. Some had even developed sore throats from breathing the dry air through our mouths. We had experienced all these discomforts for a few hours. What must it be like after a few weeks!

There was nothing for it but to go to bed. Lois was sufficiently strong-minded to make her family clean their teeth in some freezing water, but we Hillarys maintained much lower standards. With a slight feeling of guilt we put on every bit of clothing we possessed and then crawled into our double-thickness sleeping bags. Outside, the Sherpas were still dashing around with their shirt sleeves rolled up.

"I'd better show you how to do yourselves up properly in your sleeping bags," said Ed as he pulled the drawcords very tightly together so only our noses could be seen. I had an intense feeling of claustrophobia but decided that this was less important than being cold.

As the pleasant warmth of our sleeping bags revived us,

the Hillary girls and their father started singing songs about "Ten Green Bottles" walking up the glacier and falling into crevasses and such like, and before long the whole camp was singing as well. Even the Sherpas joined in when they could. We sang lustily for a couple of hours, but gradually the singing became more spasmodic as some of the little ones dropped off to sleep. Finally the camp became completely silent, gripped in an icy Himalayan hand.

CHAPTER 10

Base Camp Conquered

....

"It's been snowing inside the tent!" said Sarah.

"Don't knock the walls or there'll be a snowstorm," cautioned Ed.

"What is it really? It can't be snow," said Peter.

"It's frozen condensation," said Ed. "See, it's all round the top of your sleeping bag from your breathing."

"What's condensation?" asked Sarah.

"I'll tell you at breakfast, when I feel a bit stronger."

"I didn't sleep a wink all night," said Belinda, who up until now had been fast asleep and who looked surprisingly fresh after her first night at over fifteen thousand feet. Sarah and I were a bit of a mess, both our faces being puffy from some strange reaction to our environment. Lois called out that she was the same.

This was adventure indeed. So much so that it inspired everybody to action and we hurriedly dressed and rushed outside, where we found our ever-faithful Sherpas in the process of lighting a fire. It was hard to keep warm at first but then the blessed sun appeared and life started anew. Our appetites were a trifle jaded so we hurried through breakfast and got on with the job of packing up the camp. Two of the porters were no longer needed so they were

paid off and sent down valley. The two yaks were most
reluctant to be loaded and galloped over the hillside like
frisky clowns in a circus. Their owner was a middle-aged
and serious Sherpa with a sweet and kindly face. We
called him Pangboche Pong (Pong means "smell"), although of course this wasn't his real name. Four years
previously he had worked for Ed as a porter, and had
worn a pair of ancient sheepskin trousers with the wool
side turned in. You could smell the trousers coming
from quite a distance so the nickname Pangboche Pong
had seemed very appropriate. On this trip he was wearing a pair of ordinary woolen trousers and smelled quite
pleasant by Sherpa standards. Poor Pangboche Pong had
a terrible time catching his yaks and when we were ready
to leave camp he had just started to load up the wayward
beasts.

It was only a morning's walk to our next camp, but it
took all our energy. We puffed our way up the first long
hill, extending our lungs to the limit. The weather was
cold but perfect and all around us were incredibly high
snow peaks with tall graceful Pumori as the centerpiece.
Across the glacier Nuptse and Lhotse were fantastic sights,
terribly steep and with great bands of white strata across
their faces. Behind them we could see the top of Everest,
with a lazy plume of snow blowing out from its summit.

Poor Everest, it is only its stupendous height that makes
it famous. I have now seen it from a number of angles
and it has never looked anything but an ugly, ungraceful
lump, a real country cousin among the beautiful peaks surrounding it. Yet there is something rather terrifying about
its dark brooding shape.

By thinking only of the next step ahead we dragged ourselves up a steep rise to where the track lost itself in the
wild shifting moraine of a tributary glacier. For an hour

we stumbled across loose rock and slippery ice and up onto
the moraine wall on the other side. From here we could
see our next camp site, still some distance away.

Lake Camp or Gorakshep, as it was called by the local
people, was a glorious retreat from the high mountains
around the Khumbu glacier. On one side was a pleasant
grassy slope, which protected the camp from many of the
violent winds. On the other side was a lovely lake, frozen
at this time of the year. Ed had first camped at Gorakshep fifteen years before and it has always been a special
resting place for Everest expeditions, being only a few
hours' walk from the icefall leading to the Western Cwm.

As we approached this pleasant retreat, strength seemed
to flow back into our legs and we ran toward the exotic
high-altitude skating rink. Mike Gill was the first to
sally out on the ice. Looking like a Russian author of in-
tellectual novels, he slid across the surface, elegantly pro-
pelling himself with his carefully folded umbrella. The
children rushed after him with screams of delight and before long the lake was covered with cavorting people shouting and laughing as they slid and fell on icy reflections of
Mount Everest. It was a truly mad scene and even the
Sherpas became infected and found boxes and sacks and ice
axes with which to propel the young Hillarys and Pearls
across the ice.

I had been rather wary of venturing on the lake, being
quite convinced I would fall flat on my face. Ed in gallant
fashion offered to escort me across. We shuffled our way
along without incident until we reached the center of the
lake when suddenly we heard horrible abrupt creaking
noises, almost like gunshots. They were coming from somewhere in our vicinity and the touching little picture of husband and wife happily crossing the ice hand in hand was
shattered as I rushed wildly for the shore, leaving Ed stand-

ing there in mild surprise. We discovered later that during
the hottest part of the day the ice cracked and contorted,
due presumably to the heat of the sun.

While we were skating, Ang Passang was digging desperately in the steely surface of the lake for drinking water.
It was at least half an hour before he could chop his way
through to a sufficient supply for our large party, but once
this was done lunch was soon ready. We ate thin packet
soup and boiled potatoes that were very firm in the center
due to the reduced boiling point of water at this altitude.
No one cared too much about food anyway and quite a few
of us were feeling a little off color.

The energetic members of the party decided to go for a
walk toward the slopes of Pumori. It was from Pumori in
1951 that Ed and Eric Shipton, the well-known British ex-
plorer, had first looked into the Western Cwm and seen the
answer to the route up Everest. From our Gorakshep
camp the icefall and Western Cwm were still completely
hidden and it was easy to understand why this side of Everest had been considered unclimbable.

"It's just an hour or two across the moraine," said Ed.
"It'll be wonderful to go back and have a look." I reminded
him that in those days he had been much younger and
much fitter and that he was now taking his wife and only
son on this "walk." Quite undismayed he explained that
he had brought all the necessary equipment, and I noticed
that the Sherpas who were going to accompany us were
bristling with ice axes and ropes. Under normal conditions
I would have retreated to my tent on seeing such alarming equipment, but for once my well-submerged sense of
adventure came to the fore. Here I was at 16,500 feet on
the slopes of Mount Everest. It had taken a great deal of
effort to get there, and I was unlikely ever to return, so I
just had to take part in every possible activity.

The first part of our walk was up a steep three-hundred-foot grassy hill to the top of the moraine. On various occasions I decided to give in but to my amazement soon found that I was keeping up with the party very well. From the top we could see a desert of jumbled rocks ahead of us. Moraine ridges that looked like fearsome ocean swells turned the scene into wild chaos. A black spur leading up toward Pumori was pointed out as our objective. It was miles away and completely unobtainable—there just weren't enough hours left in the day. Even though quite outnumbered, I pointed out the craziness of the scheme and suggested an attractive rock peak pushing up through the moraine only half the distance away. My luck was in, and permission was granted.

Up and down, over the shaking and shifting piles of rock, we scrambled.

"I can't go on," I'd say to myself. "This is absolute madness. I'll never make it to the top of the next ridge." But somehow or other I always did. Twice while we were puffing our way across the moraine we heard the cannon-like boom of an avalanche cascading and billowing its way down the lower slopes of Nuptse to the Khumbu glacier below. Soon after there would be a wild gust of wind whipping clouds of dust around us, and changing the already chaotic scene into a nightmare.

On the ridge that led to our peak we were allowed a short rest and this gave me a chance to have a good look at our little band. We were rather a strange group to be in such a place. Peter and myself were complete greenhorns, and Ed, a climber of Everest; Mike Gill had done some of the finest climbing on the steep and difficult mountains of the Everest region; Max had clawed his way up to nineteen thousand on Mount Tamserku two years previously without any climbing experience; and our two young builders, Brian and Stuart, were avid climbers in the New Zealand Alps. Our Sherpas included Pemba Tarkay, one of the finest of all high-altitude climbers; his constant companion, Siku, a tough and cheerful mountaineer; the vigorous and hardy Phu Dorje; and the tall reliable Tenzing Niendra with perhaps the greatest potential of them all. Then there was Mingma, vastly experienced in leadership and organization, reliable and loyal. Here was a group that could have carried *me* to the top of Everest, and instead our objective was a heap of stony rubble in the middle of the glacier.

I couldn't help laughing at the incongruity of it all, but it wasn't a laughing matter for the Sherpas. For two years the Nepalese Government had banned all foreign climbing expeditions mainly because of complaints from the Chinese Government that expeditions (not necessarily mountaineering ones) had illegally crossed the border into Tibet. Employment on expeditions had been a valuable source of finance for the Sherpas and the loss of it was making life very difficult. When Ed was recruiting Sherpas to do various jobs on the hospital and for our Everest trek he was overwhelmed with requests for work from every ablebodied Sherpa in the district.

But to me, at that moment, this eighteen-thousand-foot hill was the challenge of my life. The last five hundred feet to the summit was steep but not at all difficult—in fact, there were patches of moss and occasional wisps of grass all the way up.

"If I stop halfway for a rest," I said, "I'll never start again." So, after heaving myself to my feet, I walked slowly but determinedly upward. Ed led the way and sent the Sherpas to find a good and very easy route for the Memsahib. They dashed around the mountain as though they were playing games near the Khunde hospital. Every now and then they would appear with cheerful grins on their faces and make suggestions as to where I should put my feet. I went on up, not daring to look above or below until, on the only really steep piece of rock, my breath just seemed to desert me. Everything became a little gray and fuzzy in front of my eyes and I decided that it was time to sit down. There was nowhere suitable for sitting, but I found a crack in the rock that fitted me quite well.

"What's the matter?" Ed yelled from above.

"Oh, I just feel a little wuzzy," I said. Ed and the Sherpas immediately came rushing down toward me.

"I'm okay. Just seem to have lost my breath," I reassured them. Max asked me if I needed medical aid and I felt pleasantly fussed over. I soon felt better and signified my ability to continue.

"Keep an eye on the Memsahib," Mingma and Ed ordered, and we started up again. The Sherpas formed a circle around me and more or less propelled me upward by pushing and pulling. The last little section was really quite steep but at least there were plenty of good handholds to grab. Peter was panting very deeply and had clearly lost most of his enthusiasm, but he plodded on up in determined fashion. I hardly noticed when we reached the top. I was too involved in breathing and the effort of walking—all I wanted to do was have a rest.

Mike was busy with the movie camera down below us.

"Walk across to the lower peak," he yelled. "I can get a good picture of you from there." It was one of those nasty little exposed ridges with nothing to hold on to.

"No!" I called out, but I was quickly silenced and hauled along to sit silhouetted against Pumori while the camera buzzed busily to record this important ascent.

Back on the summit slabs of rock, I wandered about intoxicated with success.

"I think you had better sit down for a minute or two," someone suggested rather dampeningly. I sat down and drank in the incredible sight that met my eyes. Below us was the Khumbu glacier, which swept out from the wild chaotic icefall. It was dotted with sharp toothlike ice séracs that looked tiny from our position, but some of them must have been fifty to one hundred feet high. Among them Ed pointed out the position of Everest Base Camp, now a long way below us. Up to the left of the icefall was the steep Lho La, a mountain pass into Tibet. It looked very close and over it we could see some of the mountains of that strange and forbidden land. When the Indian expedition climbed Mount Everest the year before, there were Chinese observers on the Lho La the whole time watching their progress. I wondered if we were being watched at this very moment.

Above the icefall we could look into the Western Cwm, the snowy valley that is the key to the climb of Everest from the south. High above it was the famous South Col (25,800 feet), the dreaded camping place of all Everest climbers before they tackle the last few thousand feet of the mountain. Finally there was the peak of Everest, large, bulky, and indestructible, with its plume of snow blowing off the summit.

A frantic amount of photographing then ensued. I took shot after shot, as I doubted if I would ever climb an 18,300-foot mountain again. Why was it that the best places to stand for photographs were always on the edges of terrifying drops? Mike decided to take some more movies of the Hillary family saga and asked all the other people on the summit to get down out of sight. Max crawled quietly under an overhanging rock, but the exuberant Phu Dorje had to be chased away by Mike. As soon as the filming was completed everyone reappeared again as if by magic.

The sun was dipping down behind the ridge and it was high time we started the journey back if we were to reach camp before dark.

"Where's Max?" I said.

"Yes, where's Max?" said Peter and Ed and everybody else. We all looked around and finally found Max, still hiding underneath his boulder and unaware that the filming had stopped some time before.

We had decided to descend a smooth consolidated gravel slope on the other side of the peak. I realized it was steep because you could look almost straight down on a delightful frozen lake a thousand feet below. But it was very easy going and I felt unconcerned. Suddenly I noticed I wasn't traveling alone, for a stout Sherpa had appeared on either side of me. Mingma must have thought that I might stumble and fall into the icy depths of the glacier lake and was taking precautions. I was a little lightheaded, I must admit, due to my recent success on my Himalayan peak. Finally Mingma offered me his ice axe.

"You had better use this," he said.

"Oh, no, it's all right, Mingma," I replied.

"No, you must use it, Burrah Memsahib. Hold it across your body with the point going into the slope so that if you fall you can stop yourself."

Feeling like a naughty schoolgirl out on a Sunday picnic, I decided to do as I was told. Poor Mingma would have found it much easier to escort some hardy mountaineers up a high Himalayan peak than nurse me down a slippery heap of stones.

When we were safely back on the moraine Ed asked Mingma to send Sherpas ahead to find a quick way back to camp. They discovered an excellent route and we romped along, reveling in the soft evening light as the sun dropped behind the graceful mountains on our right. Because it was early winter, we had seen none of the lovely Himalayan flowers, but on this barren desertlike moraine we came across little clumps of dainty blue poppies that had been deep frozen, thus retaining their perfect shape and color. Knowing my weakness for flowers, Mingma picked me a handful, which I carried carefully all the way back to camp.

A huge glowing fire welcomed us at Gorakshep. We had carried a few loads of firewood up from the lower valley and these were being supplemented by dry yak dung and little clumps of yellow moss. My homecoming wasn't completely cheerful, for Lois had put a very miserable Sarah to bed. I placed the precious paperlike poppies beside our tent and went in to see the invalid.

Poor Sarah was misery personified, with her pale face poking out of her sleeping bag and highlighted by an extremely red and sunburned nose.

"How are you?" I said.

A pathetic little voice answered, "Not very well, Mum." She had an unpleasant headache, nausea, and a sort of chesty cold.

"I'll have a look at her," Max said, poking his head into the tent. After a careful examination he gave me a handful of pills. "These will steady her stomach," he said, putting a couple of tiny white pills in my hand, "and these aspirins should fix her headaches. Then I think you had better give her some of these, as she seems to have a bit of an infection."

"Goodness me," I thought, "everything seems to be wrong with Sarah."

Long before we arrived in the Himalayas I had been worried about the possible effect of high altitude on the children. Now it had happened. The only amusing side to the situation was the thoroughly basic method of handing out the pills. Max poured them into my grubby hand and I calmly popped them into my pocket along with a jumble of handkerchiefs, lip salve, and goodness knows what. Cleanliness somehow didn't seem quite so important up here.

"Well, Sarah, you'll be all right," I said in my most cheerful bedside fashion. "How about taking some of these pills?"

"No!"

"Why not?" I asked.

"I'm going to be sick."

"Hold on a minute then," I said to her, as I hurriedly departed toward the cooking fire.

"Have you any suitable tins to be sick into?" I inquired of the Sherpas. After a hasty look around, Ang Passang offered me an empty peach can. I hurried back and was just in time to field poor Sarah's lunch. In a little while she looked much better, but her headache was obviously worrying her. I gave her the aspirin and she began to look much more comfortable.

Ed offered to sleep outside the tent that night so that there would be more room for me to move about and attend to Sarah, but in the end there didn't seem to be any need for this. I managed to put the peach tin in a strategic position and we all tied ourselves up carefully in our sleeping bags, like a collection of giant mummies. Even with the help of sleeping tablets I didn't sleep a minute during the night and so became aware of the strange noises and activity around us. All night the yaks wandered about the camp with their bells tinkling, while now and then I'd hear a sharp crack as the ice in the lake expanded with the cold. More exciting was the roar of avalanches off

Nuptse and then the resultant violent gusts of wind which came tearing down our little valley.

It was all very eerie and strange. To add to it Sarah was breathing very heavily and Peter was doing a spasmodic Cheyne Stoke type of breathing which I found most unnerving. He would breathe hard for three or four breaths and then suddenly stop and I would lie there waiting and wondering what was going to happen, until there would be a deep shuddering breath and he would continue in the same pattern. Luckily, Ed and Belinda seemed to breathe normally all night and I was most thankful for this. As I lay there I found my deep, rapid breathing in the cold air was making my throat quite sore. By three o'clock I had a severe altitude headache and a congested throat and could stand it no longer. I didn't want to wake the family, but I sat up, had a good cough, groped around the tent and found a mug of water and some aspirins. After breaking the ice off the water and making a dreadful clatter in the process, I swallowed my pills and sank back exhausted into my sleeping bag. Thank goodness I managed an hour's pleasant doze before morning.

Sarah was much better and Peter lived through the night despite his strange breathing. Lois and I felt thoroughly worn out, but it's amazing what a cup of hot tea mixed with lumpy dehydrated milk can do, and we soon felt reasonably revitalized.

This was the day we planned to venture forth onto the Khumbu glacier and walk to the famous Everest Base Camp. Ice axes and ropes were produced and we dressed in our toughest boots and warmest clothing. Sarah said she was better, but for breakfast she had only a crystallized apricot and a drink of lemon.

We had been traveling for twenty minutes when Sarah

suddenly stopped, with tears pouring down her cheeks. "I can't go on," she said most tragically.

"We'll have you carried," said Ed, and all the Sherpas agreed that this was a fine idea, but it was quite clear after a little while that the poor child was feeling so nauseated that the trip would turn into a nightmare for her if she continued. Sadly we accepted the fact that not all the Hillary family would make it to Base Camp that day, and with Sarah sitting comfortably on Ang Dawa's shoulders I departed with her back down the track to camp.

A strong cold wind was blowing down the valley, but the sun was streaming into the tent, making it warm and snug. Sarah sat down on the comfortable thickness of four sleeping bags and I propped her up with a few more behind her back so that she looked utterly relaxed. The warmth and comfort soon cheered her up and we had a pleasant lazy morning. The kindly Sherpas kept bringing us cups of thin soup and tea, and to pass the time we played cards and drew pictures while the porters sat in rows two and three deep watching us. Beyond the porters was an interested audience of two large ungainly Himalayan choughs—members of the crow family—who stared at us unwaveringly for a couple of hours.

"What would you like for lunch?" said Ang Tsering.

"Oh, nothing much," I said disinterestedly.

"I want something," said Sarah, and immediately Ang Tsering's face beamed with joy to think that she was feeling better.

"I'd like lots of potatoes," she said, "and lots of butter and lots of cheese."

"Good heavens," I gasped, "you can't eat all that when you've been feeling so sick."

"Oh, yes I can," she said.

A few minutes later we were brought a large pile of the

little local potatoes that had been boiled in their skins. They had been boiled for an hour or more and were completely cooked. Sarah ate her first potato rather gingerly, but she added lumps of butter and cheese to the next ones and ate them with great enjoyment.

I had been told repeatedly that it was useless to sit around and just wait for your body to get used to high altitudes, so, as Sarah looked much stronger after her meal, I suggested we go for a walk along the moraine wall to view the tall séracs that seemed to dance so crazily along the surface of the Khumbu glacier. As a precaution I decided to take one of the Sherpas and asked Ang Tsering if he knew his way to Base Camp.

"Yes, I know the way," he replied very quietly.

"Could you come with us then?"

"Yes, Memsahib. Right away."

We walked up toward the moraine and I asked Ang Tsering if he had been to Everest Base Camp before. "Yes, about twenty times, Memsahib," he replied. I nearly collapsed with astonishment, for Ang Tsering is rather portly and does not look like a mountaineer.

"Have you been to the South Col?" I said.

"Yes, Memsahib, about seven or eight times."

I gasped but continued walking. "Have you been higher?"

"Oh, yes, Memsahib. I have carried to the final camp." What an amazing and unassuming character he was.

"When did you first go to Everest?" I asked next.

"In 1953 with the Burrah Sahib."

"Good heavens!" I said. "I never knew that. Does the Burrah Sahib know it?"

"No, I have never told him."

"How old were you?" I asked, quickly doing some mental arithmetic, because even though Ang Tsering looked unathletic he was not very old.

"I was sixteen," he said, "and I carried three times to the South Col on that expedition." Well, at least Sarah and I were in good hands. I was bursting to tell Ed all this news but could see no sign of the returning Base Camp party. We sat on a little moss-covered ridge in the sun until Ang Tsering saw them coming and asked if he could leave us, knowing that we would be quite safe.

"I have much work to do," he said. "The potatoes must be peeled and there are other preparations for dinner that must be done." Ang Tsering typified all that was best in the Sherpas—so very gentle, so very strong and tough, a leader of men in his own community but quite happy to work with young Sherpa boys at peeling the potatoes for dinner. I found out later than many mountaineering expeditions think that Ang Tsering is one of the best sirdars in Nepal.

The Base Camp party returned in varying stages of exhaustion and elation. First came Belinda, holding hard to Siku's hand. He must have pulled her and carried her at great speed all the way down the glacier. Next came Tenzing Niendra and Ang Dawa, carrying huge loads of timber that had been used for bridging crevasses on one of the earlier Everest expeditions—this timber was going to make a fire for us. Then came Peter and Ed looking rather worn but quite pleased with themselves, and close on their heels, the rest of the party who were in about the same conditions, except for young Susan who had been stricken by the altitude and was feeling weak and sad. Susan walked stoically back to camp and was put into a warm sleeping bag to recuperate, but it wasn't long before her big sisters came to ask for a lend of the empty peach can for their poor nauseated sister.

A fierce gusty wind started to blow whirlwinds of dust down the Lake Camp valley, making it almost impossible to sit beside the fire. As we played musical chairs with the wind and tried not to be burned by sudden tongues of flame, the day's outing was discussed.

"It was a terrific slog," said Ed.

"It's very much farther than it looks," said one of the tired children. But the fascinations of the gleaming ice séracs and the eerie atmosphere created by the tattered remains of many Everest expeditions had made the day a great adventure. One of the more energetic Base Camp walkers had returned with a couple of souvenirs—an old battered Swiss primus stove and a broken radio.

When the meal appeared, our appetites fled, and the winds continued blowing even harder until they nearly blew our great fire away.

"Well, I'm going to bed," said one of the more sensible members of the party. We all followed suit. Before going to my tent I made preparations to ensure a good night's sleep. First I found a large Chinese thermos belonging to one of the Sherpas and filled it with hot lemon drink to sooth our parched throats. Then I procured a very stiff dose of sleeping tablets for myself, as I was quite determined to have some sleep. After a great deal of complicated jockeying around, trying to find places for the thermos, our handkerchiefs, torches, and all manner of other things, we managed to squeeze ourselves into our thick bags. As I lay in bed I realized that my clothing had become completely permeated with the choking acrid fumes from the yak dung fire. The smell was very strong but not unpleasant, and I gradually slid into a peaceful sleep.

CHAPTER 11

Christmas in Sherpaland

....

When we poked our noses out of the tent in the morning it was obvious we had just completed our Base Camp trip in time. Wild clouds were scurrying across the tops of the peaks and violent winds came shrieking down the Khumbu glacier, hitting our tents with such resounding force that I was amazed that they stood up to the strain. It was extremely cold, so everyone ran to the wildly glowing fire and put their boots beside it to thaw out. Greedy tongues of flame came reaching out and set fire to the laces, so the indestructible Phu Dorje leaped into the inferno and saved our footwear.

Susan had come stumbling out of her tent looking a woebegone little figure. She hadn't eaten for twenty-four hours, and couldn't keep any liquid in her stomach. Sarah, our other invalid, said she had recovered, but looked a washed-out, puffy-eyed little adventurer. As for myself, I was thankful that no one had a mirror, for I knew my nose was bright scarlet, my eyes puffy, my hair stiff with dirt, and my clothes decidedly bedraggled. Of course we were all in the same condition, so no one had any grounds for complaint.

We forced our stiff boots onto our frozen feet and started on the homeward trek with hardly a backward glance at Everest, which was now wreathed in an angry diadem of scuffling gray clouds.

"Perhaps we'll have a white Christmas," said some of the younger members of the party in great excitement. We looked up at the racing clouds and willed them to become worse and worse, for it was the twenty-fourth of December and the New Zealanders of the party had never experienced the traditional snowy Christmas of the northern hemisphere.

The three older children hurried on ahead in very bouncing fashion, winding their way through the moraine of the tributary glacier with complete confidence. The younger ones found the walking much more of an effort, but it was amazing to see the gradual improvement in their attitude to life as we steadily dropped down the valley. Once again, faithful Mingma had his Sherpas scurrying about the track protecting us from any harm. In an amazingly short time we reached the terminal face of the Khumbu glacier and made a wild dash five hundred feet down the broad grassy slope as life seeped back into our sluggish bodies. It was a strange sensation coming down to more human levels again. We became quite lighthearted and scurried effortlessly downhill, greedily breathing in the earthy smells, the scent of grass, and the softer balmy air. It was marvelous to relax in our breakfast spot at 14,500 feet and bask in the warm sunshine again.

To celebrate our return from rarefied atmospheres I persuaded my family to clean their teeth. With a further display of energy we brought out our diaries, which hadn't been touched for several days. The Sherpas too made a great show of cleanliness and washed their hands, faces, and hair in the icy stream. But hunger put a stop to all this activity, and we demolished three or four boxes of cereal with warm milk. It was one of the most delicious repasts we had had for some time.

"Come on, don't dally around," we were told, "you've got to do two and a half days' walk in one, as the Head Lama is expecting us at Thyangboche tonight." This sounded far worse than it really was, for on the homeward journey we would be walking downhill nearly all the time. After our meal the speed increased a hundred per cent, as we went thumping down the wide and glorious alpine valley. Siku was in the lead, with the three older children, and headed across the valley and over acres of stunted shrubs that were still clothed in brilliant autumn coloring. Da Nimi, one of the porters, then led us along the side of the valley among delightful little meadows and between great boulders, until we came to an exquisite little sheltered corner where there were three or four velvety meadows enclosed by high stone walls and with a cosy little stone cottage in one corner. We sat down for a rest and Da Nimi looked very self-conscious and proud as he leaned against the house.

"What a lovely place," I said to Mingma. "I wonder who lives here."

"This is Da Nimi's house," was the reply. "He brings his yaks to graze here in the summer." I am sure that no king, president, or millionaire has such a beautiful summer residence as Da Nimi. The view took in all the high peaks of the Everest area, and below we could see the wild Imja river, bordered by forests and yak pastures, as it stretched away into the distance. We rushed down the hillside toward the river and went swiftly along the track that led to the village of Pangboche. As we approached the village we noticed that Peter had finally got tired of girls' company and was striding ahead at great speed with young Nima, aged fifteen, the cook's assistant. They were chatting busily together while easily outstripping the rest of the party.

On the outskirts of Pangboche we were met by some of the village elders, who invited us to inspect the school that Ed had built for them four years before. As the school was a good two hundred feet above our track the idea was not very popular, but an official visit to the school was expected of us, so with much effort we stopped our strong downward trend and changed gear into upward motion. The school was in fine order and the views magnificent, but we were a drooping and unappreciative party.

"Why aren't the Sahibs taking pictures?" asked the Pangboche men. "All Sahibs take many pictures." But we were no longer in the mood for photography and trooped wearily down the hill on the dusty track. All the inhabitants of the village were waiting to welcome us at the Gompa, and already the deep Tibetan trumpets were sounding and all the village dogs barking in chorus.

"I wonder what they want?" Ed murmured to himself. "They have a school, they have a teacher. Ah! I know," he said with sudden conviction, "they want a new roof for their Gompa!"

"Well, it's very nice of them to put on such a welcome," I called back as I hurried down to receive their openhearted hospitality.

When I arrived at the Gompa a friendly crowd of villagers surrounded me and I turned on my most appreciative and happy smile. I was thoroughly enjoying myself when my gracious act was ruthlessly disturbed.

"Hurry up. Come back!" said Ed.

"You can't do that," I called back. "It would be very rude to walk out on such a delightful gathering."

"Come on and don't waste time," he repeated. So I hurriedly retreated and was told that Ed was quite determined the Pangboche people should bring their welcome to a sunny corner of the village where we could talk in warmth and comfort. The whole party then set off toward a sunlit courtyard, and we were soon followed by all the people, the Tibetan trumpets, the dogs, various pieces of furniture, and the ever-present large containers of chung and rakshi and other liquid refreshment.

"Let's have a good meal, quickly!" I said to the Sherpas as these menacing bottles appeared. "At least we'll have something inside our stomachs to protect us." We hastily munched stale cabin biscuits spread with honey or peanut butter and felt a little better prepared to meet our public. The head men of the village advanced upon us first. They were a rough, cheerful, and piratical lot, most with the long traditional plaits of hair wound round their heads and cocky Tibetan hats placed rakishly on top. The leader of the band sported a wispy, long mustache, for like all Mongolians he had very little facial hair. His few treasured whiskers gave him the expression of a wily old tomcat. For every drink we had, the head men drank two or three, and by the time the speeches started these leading citizens were rather unsteady on their feet.

"Our Gompa is the oldest one in the area," they said. "This building is very important to us, for it is the focal point of our village life and the great Guru Rimpoche passed by here many hundreds of years ago. Burrah Sahib, please replace our old shingle roof with aluminum. You are the father of us all, you are our protector." They were really making a fuss over the Burrah Sahib and enjoying every moment of it. But Ed wasn't very happy with the village; in fact, he was decidedly grumpy. "Why has the attendance at your school been so bad this year? If you can't use your school properly, why should I help you with a Gompa roof?"

Two trainee nurses in hospital surgery.

Dr. McKinnon, the Sherpa nurse Yung-
en, and Dianne McKinnon stop for
norning tea in the dispensary.

Edmund Hillary is made welcome at a
Sherpa school with gifts of katas (white
scarves), and various drinks—from left,
beer, yak milk, and rakshi, a superpotent
Sherpa brew.

Louise Hillary entertains Kappa Kalden and wife in the Long Stay Ward.

The Thyroid Research group plan their day's operation at Phortse. With them are villagers from this isolated community who are deformed by cretinism.

From 18,300 feet, the man who conquered Everest, his son and wife, look up at it . . .

Sarah and Belinda Hillary and Susan Pearl prepare to leave for the Everest base camp, while an unidentified local girl looks on.

. . . And, looking down, from their own peak.

A man and his son. Sir Edmund Hillary and Peter stand on the site of the base camp from which the successful assault on Everest was made in 1953.

Mountain men. From left: Ang Tsering, Mingma Tsering, Siku, Ang Pema.

Thyangboche monastery.

The man who climbed Everest is climbed himself, by his own team.

They all looked very sad and downcast at this comment and many were the explanations and excuses, and promises. Finally Ed relented a little. "If you make a great effort to send your children to school next year, then perhaps there might be some way of raising money for the necessary aluminum. But the school must come first!" Immediately their faces brightened and after much discussion and much ceremonial scarf-giving we were free to continue on our way.

The track wound along the precipitous sides of the river. After the Pangboche party, Mingma seemed quite sure that I would be feeling a little unsteady on my feet, so he walked exactly twelve inches behind me. We came to the steep hill below Thyangboche. Suddenly I felt completely exhausted, more exhausted than I had been for a long time. I could see the graceful roof of the monastery through the trees, and I pictured myself sitting by the little stove in the Thyangboche guesthouse, relaxed and warm.

Just then Nima came running down the track with a wicked grin on his face.

"American men in guesthouse," he said cheerfully, knowing full well the chaos that would ensue. I groaned to myself as my dreams of comfort were dashed to the ground. Nima continued down the track, telling everyone the sad news.

But at the guesthouse things had been happening. The Head Lama on hearing of our arrival had sent his brother, a most impressive and businesslike young man, to the American family to tell them they would have to move. They were in the midst of cooking dinner and could hardly believe their ears, but the Head Lama's brother was quite firm about the matter. I arrived in the guesthouse grounds to see their fire and their pots of half-cooked food being moved across the meadow to the colorful but drafty school building. My relief at seeing the guesthouse vacated was forgotten when I saw the forlorn family and all their belongings drifting rather sadly around the yak pasture.

"I'm terribly sorry about this," I said in great embarrassment.

"Oh, that's perfectly all right," they replied gallantly. "We know you have a prior claim, as your husband donated timber to the guesthouse."

"Come and have dinner," I said rather lamely as the last of their half-cooked food disappeared across the field.

"Oh no, we wouldn't bother you like that," they said. "We'll be fine. By the way, we brought a present for your children," and they produced a large tin of sweets.

This was almost the final blow, to think that these thoughtful folk had come up here with a present for the Pearl and Hillary families only to be thrown out of the guesthouse as a reward. My guilt was unbearable.

"You must come and have coffee with us after dinner," I said rather desperately. "You can sit by the warm fire."

"Thanks a lot, we would love that," they said as they departed.*

Soon the guesthouse was filled with the noisy thumping of air mattresses being inflated and other preparations being made. The new cast-iron stove installed by Ed a couple of weeks before was glowing a cherry red and it was all incredibly warm and comfortable.

We still had to pay our respects to the Head Lama. Mingma showed us the way by the light of a pressure lamp that had lost its glass and flared in weird and dangerous fashion in the cold night air. The Head Lama's

---

* We found out later that our new friends lived in Katmandu, where the father was employed by U. S. Aid, and that they had decided to visit Thyangboche during their Christmas holiday.

private room was lined with religious books and beautiful images of the Buddha. We sat on benches covered with handsome Tibetan rugs and were warmed by a charcoal brazier, which glowed in the middle of the floor. The now mildly flaring pressure lamp cast a soft and flickering light over the scene. Being a very understanding and practical man, the Head Lama ordered Indian tea for the younger members of our party. This was served in dainty English teacups decorated with rosebuds. The children drank many cups and ate an enormous number of special party biscuits that had obviously been given to the Head Lama by some expedition. Then it was the parents' turn and we were offered Tibetan tea, or rakshi out of a shapely antique Chinese porcelain jug.

I decided on Tibetan tea. Even though I have never enjoyed it, it was definitely the lesser of two evils. To my surprise I found myself sipping the tea with pleasure, for it was a good hot brew. Tibetan tea is a strange drink to our palates. The tea leaves are processed by a different method and shaped into large bricks. A chunk of tea is boiled in water for several minutes and strained into a large wooden churn, where yak butter—usually rancid—and a little salt is added. This mixture is vigorously and thoroughly mixed, and the resultant flavor is like thin, moldy soup. We were also offered delicious thin potato chips fried in butter. They had been garnished with finely chopped onion leaves and we ate greedily. Then we took our leave, after extracting a promise from the Head Lama that he would join us in the guesthouse for dinner.

As always, our guest was incredibly prompt. In fact, he appeared fifteen minutes before the arranged time.

"Hurry up with the food, Ang Passang," I called, for the Head Lama was a restless visitor and hated to sit around making polite conversation.

When the meal was over I suggested that the children sing some New Zealand songs. The Head Lama enjoyed them very much, but we soon exhausted our repertoire.

"It's Christmas Eve," the children chorused. "Let's sing carols."

We adults wondered at the reaction of our devout Buddhist host but we all agreed that he wouldn't mind. In fact, he had been so curious about Christianity when we talked to him on previous occasions that we felt he would welcome the idea. So for the next half hour the sound of Christmas carols drifted around the Buddhist monastery of Thyangboche while the tall prayer flags flapped in the breeze and the Head Lama sat in front of our fire with a happy and contented smile on his face. When he rose to take his leave we peered outside the door in hopes of seeing signs of snow, but the sky was clear and the little Sherpa world slumbered peacefully.

"Off to bed, all of you," said both fathers, and Ed added, "you won't find any Christmas stockings tomorrow morning when you wake."

"We don't care," all the children replied. "This Himalayan holiday is the most wonderful Christmas present that anyone could ever have."

We didn't escape entirely from the family traditions of Christmas, for in the early hours of next morning we could hear cheerful cries of "Happy Christmas" echoing round the guesthouse. What a happy Christmas it was! Even the weather was doing its best for us. In the early morning, strange billowing clouds rose up from the valley floor and sprinkled us with snowflakes. By the time the sun was up it was clear and brilliant. We ran outside and became quite ecstatic over the sight that met our eyes. Every branch and twig sparkled with snow crystals and frost, the mountains were dazzling white and sharp against the deep purity of the sky, and the Thyangboche monastery seemed to float above an ebbing tide of soft morning mist. In our immediate foreground ten silky-haired yaks munched busily at the hoary grass, while dotted around the meadow were yak-sized frostless patches that gave evidence of the places in which they had spent the night.

Immediately after breakfast we were escorted to the monastery, where the Head Lama was waiting for us beside an overhanging rock. With great pride he showed us his flower garden—really just a hole in the ground with a clear plastic sheet over it and a heavy wooden lid to keep out the frost at night. Despite the cold and the altitude, he had miniature roses blooming, calendulas and geraniums, and to my delight he picked one of his precious flowers and gave it to me.

With the Head Lama to guide us, we visited the two great temple rooms of the monastery with their collections of sacred books and magnificent images of the Buddha and the Guru Rimpoche. Every inch of the walls and ceilings was covered with beautifully executed and brilliantly colored religious paintings. The numerous scroll paintings and decorative silk hangings created a rich and impressive atmosphere. On a shelf near the ceiling were a number of exquisite little images, but the Head Lama told us in sorrow that the collection was now incomplete, as several of the pieces had been stolen. High prices were being paid by tourists in Katmandu for such images, and this had precipitated a wave of thefts from lamas and temples. The cold started to gnaw into my bones and I marveled at the Head Lama with his arms bare to the shoulder and his highly disciplined control over the discomforts of the flesh.

We returned to the sunshine again and were almost blinded by the glare. The Head Lama presented us with scarves in farewell, then stood at the edge of the lovely Thyangboche meadow to wave us good-bye. He stood there for a moment, an impressive but rather lonely figure, and turned abruptly and disappeared.

We ran most of the way down the two-thousand-foot hill to the Dudh Kosi river, reveling in our energy at these lower levels. Halfway up the other side, Ang Dawa stopped to cut some fir trees for the Christmas party we were planning for the Sherpa children.

Our return to the hospital went practically unnoticed by the resident doctor, John McKinnon, and his wife Dianne. The whole place was a hive of activity, as Dianne hadn't expected us for another day and was organizing a Christmas party for the Sherpa staff and their wives. When she finally became aware of the twenty extra dinner guests, her enthusiasm was temporarily dampened. But after we had agreed that it would be a "Family Hold Back" night, the preparations continued with unabated fury. She had been busy all day baking pineapple upside-down cakes and loaves of bread, and making sophisticated-looking dips, while our Long Stay Ward had been turned into a gracious buffet dinner room. On the table, paper napkins decorated with holly leaves and Father Christmases had been set out. There was even a little dish of olives—quickly becoming quite dehydrated in the cold dry air. Two large Tibetan teapots had been filled with fruit juice, and plates, mugs, knives and forks covered most of the remaining space.

"It's going to be a traditional New Zealand Christmas dinner," Dianne said, "with slight variations, of course."

Instead of a plump roast leg of lamb there were two rather scrawny-looking legs of Tibetan sheep. There were potatoes for roasting and a pumpkin just like the ones we have with a roast dinner at home. The last remaining packets of freeze-dried peas were emptied into a pot while

Ed and Ang Pemma were not looking, and everywhere in cool places were bowls of many colored jellies and exciting-looking fruit salads.

While we were waiting for our guests, someone remembered a packet of fireworks that had been given to us by the British Embassy.

"Let's fire them off to start the party!" Peter suggested.

Someone must have told the Sherpas that, on Christmas Day, Western people give presents to one another, for many of them brought little gifts. Ang Pemma gave us a small and rather faded painting of the Wheel of Life, and Ang Passang a copper dish.

Ang Dooli came with her children, and all the other Sherpas' wives arrived with their babies, who were put in baskets on our beds. Suddenly the door was flung open and Mingma made a magnificent entrance. He had been feted by many people since his return from Base Camp and was in an expansive and genial mood. In one hand he clutched a handsome copper teapot with a couple of ceremonial scarves tied around its handle.

"I would like to make a speech," he said. Ang Dooli looked slightly alarmed. Mingma didn't have a strong head for liquor and I think the relief of bringing us all safely back from Base Camp had caused him to succumb to temptation.

"I want to thank everybody for everything," he said, with a sort of uncontrolled giggle. "This hospital very good, schools very good, Burrah Sahib very good," and as an afterthought, "all doctor sahibs very good." He then presented me with the magnificent teapot, much to my delight. Mingma seemed quite prepared to carry on with his speech but we managed to distract his attention by suggesting that everyone go outside for the fireworks display.

It was very dark in front of the building, although there was a brilliant starry sky. Ed commenced with sparklers so as not to frighten our guests, but for some reason they wouldn't light properly and produced only a few hesitant sparkles. When they lit the Catherine wheels there was no doubt about their explosive quality, and instead of pinning them to the wall they just threw them wildly about, turning the audience into a screaming, shouting mob of running people. Some of the Sherpa mothers retreated inside with their wailing babies, but everyone else became more and more enthusiastic.

The sky rockets were kept until last and provided the most spectacular display of all. The first one whizzed across the fields at a height of about thirty feet and landed in the middle of some visiting Americans' camp. We silently apologized to them. The next one leaped into the sky to a great height and exploded with brilliant bursts of color. Everyone was quite entranced. Another rocket shot with great speed and precision into the balcony of Phu Dorje's house, which also delighted the audience, except for Phu Dorje. The second-to-last rocket nearly ended in disaster, as it shot up into Mingma's face, but fortunately it did nothing worse than give him a fright. By this time almost all the inhabitants of Khunde and Khumjung had gathered outside the hospital to watch the show, and when the last rocket went up straight and true into the cold night air, everyone let off a roar of applause. We hurried back into the warmth and comfort of the ward, confident that our party had started with a bang in more ways than one.

The meal was a terrific success, and it wasn't until the last piece of pineapple upside-down cake had been carefully deposited on a plate that the hosts and hostesses could relax.

To complete the evening, it was essential to have some

dancing and before long more and more of our guests were joining in.

"Sarah, Peter, Ann, Lynn, Susan, Belinda," the Sherpas cried. "Come and dance!" And dance they did, with Mike joining in too and looking like a giant between a couple of pretty little Sherpanis.

"Just three dances," Mingma said, with a placating glance at the Burrah Sahib, who looked decidedly weary. We all laughed, for everybody knew what that meant. No Sherpa party has ever ended after three dances. By half past ten our children were so tired that they crawled thankfully into their sleeping bags, and even though the dancing and talking continued for another hour they were soon fast asleep. More and more uninvited guests seemed to find their way into the room, and the thumping and stamping of the dancers grew stronger and faster every minute. I held some of the babies so their mothers could join in the fun, but it wasn't a success. Every time I picked up a bundle it would open its eyes and burst into desperate wails, bringing its mother hurrying back from the dancing.

"Enough, enough!" Mingma suddenly called. "It's time to go home." But there was one last ceremony to be performed. All the Sherpas joined in singing a song about the hospital builders and their families and then each of us was presented with a scarf while an honoring song was sung to us. It was quite a moving gesture and made a perfect ending to an enchanting and unforgettable Christmas Day.

CHAPTER 12

A Yak for Father Christmas

．．

December 26 was Peter's twelfth birthday, but this almost passed unnoticed due to our feverish preparations for the Sherpa children's Christmas party to be held on the following day. We searched Khunde and Khumjung for a suitable area to hold the gathering and finally chose a grassy field sheltered by the Khunde chorten and prayer walls. As we returned to the hospital, I tried to think up some suitable but sensational focal point for the party.

"You know, Lois, if Sherpas were Christians they would have Father Christmas riding a yak instead of a reindeer."

"I suppose so," said Lois.

"And Max would make a wonderful Father Christmas," I continued.

"Umm . . ." was the vague reply.

"Yes, that's what we want—a yak for Father Christmas!"

I became so convinced that the success of the children's party depended upon Max and a yak, that I went and asked Mingma to find a suitable animal to carry our reluctant Father Christmas. Most of the yaks I had met so far were warlike and ferocious beasts, but Mingma seemed confident that a gentle one was readily obtainable.

"The Khunde headman has some good yaks and I know

he will lend us one," he said. "In the morning I will make sure the yak has a good meal."

This sounded a fine idea.

"Thanks," I said. "I'm sure if it's well fed it will be gentle."

"Oh, yes, Burrah Memsahib, do not worry. I will feed four yaks so that you will have more than one to choose from."

Well, that appeared to complete that arrangement, and yet I was still not completely confident about our yak supply.

It was essential that I should have some capable interpreters to explain the games and competitions to the children, so I asked the three scholarship boys, Ang Rita, Lakpa Norbu, and Mingma Norbu, to come and help me with the organization. We decided that the party should start at 11 A.M. and that the boys would have the responsibility of inviting every family in the two villages. Then we discussed the entertainment. We decided to start with Maori action songs and dances by the Hillary and Pearl families, followed by songs and dances by the Khumjung school children.

"Now what about games?" I asked the three boys. Mingma Norbu, the youngest, immediately handed me a list he had made out. They were mostly the same old competitions and games that we had used at school functions in the years gone by, proving how popular they must have been.

One of our most important tasks was to prepare two hundred little Christmas gifts for the village children. We hunted through the storeroom and unearthed some biscuits, dates, and a few nuts. We also begged some of our precious chocolate from the expedition leader and then asked all the group if they had anything spare to offer. It was quite amazing to see the pile of gifts that we collected —little plastic toys, handkerchiefs, pieces of soap, and so on—and as a last resource we had the large can of sweets that had been given to us at Thyangboche. Since all the food gifts had to be tied up in little parcels, and the shortage of paper was quite acute, we used toilet paper, paper tissues, old newspapers, and pieces of used writing paper. All the Sherpa children wanted to help and I felt like an overworked orchestral conductor as I tried desperately to keep some sort of control over my workers. By the time we had finished there were enough little parcels for every Khunde and Khumjung child. We placed all the gifts in a large bamboo basket and then started to work on the two Christmas trees that Ang Dawa had cut for us the day before. To decorate these we had to use all our imagination. With the use of some carefully hoarded bright colored paper we made paper bells and simple Japanese origami birds. These we swung from the boughs of the trees.

"We must have some stars," I said.

"Yes, we'll have a really big one at the top," said Susan. "We always do." We sat and thought about this very hard for some minutes, until finally I came up with the idea of using empty soup packets, which were lined with silver paper. It was a laborious process, for first of all we had to clean each packet, turn it inside out, and finally stick them together.

By evening all the preparations for the party were completed, so after dinner Mike presented the McKinnons with their Christmas present. It was a miniature set of roulette and we all clustered round the table and became deeply engrossed in gambling for matches, with the children very enthusiastically involved. A pressure lamp was placed beside the roulette wheel to prevent foul play and our son became so lost in the game that he leaned against the lamp and burned a hole in his precious padded jacket. He was very distressed, as the jacket was his pride and joy, but he was calmed by Ang Tsering's assurances that the garment would be patched and as good as new by morning.

Everyone was up early on December 27. Before I had time to collect my thoughts, our children had started work on the Christmas trees, which quickly took on the appearance of an overloaded clothes line. They proudly carried the decorated trees down to the Khunde chorten to await the Christmas party. I followed the trees and found Ang Rita, Lakpa Norbu, and Mingma Norbu digging a deep hole in a nearby potato field. There they placed a tall tree trunk. I asked them what it was for but received no definite explanation. They were clearly very happy, so I didn't interfere.

It was nearly eleven o'clock and our Sherpa guests were not in sight. The four gentle and well-fed yaks hadn't appeared either, and I was sure that my Christmas party was going to be a dreadful fiasco.

"Where are the yaks, Mingma?"

"In the field over there, Memsahib," he replied.

I looked in the direction that he pointed, and saw a group of twenty large staring beasts.

"Which one is it to be?" I asked nervously.

"Oh, whichever one is easy to catch." The plans seemed to have changed since the previous day.

Looking rather like a doomed gladiator, he set off with a long rope to catch a yak, while I told our children to clear the stones off the ground so that no one would trip during the races. Fascinated, I watched Mingma advance bravely toward the black-faced mob and tentatively tie the rope round the horns of one of the yaks. It immediately tossed its head, pawed the ground, and ran away. He tried another, and another, with exactly the same result. Finally there was a shout of satisfaction. He had successfully captured a yak and started to lead it up the track to the hospital. As it approached the waiting Father Christmas, who was dressed in a scarlet windproof suit complete with hoary cottonwool face and red hat—it pawed the earth, and bucked and jumped most violently. Even Max looked a little disconcerted, so Mingma let it go, much to the relief of all of us.

Another helpful villager came to our rescue with the offer of one of his yaks whose gentle temperament he completely guaranteed. But as soon as it saw Max it went quite berserk and had to be taken off to a quiet field to calm down.

It was becoming clear that the ordinary milk-producing yaks were of no use. What we needed was an experienced load-carrying yak. After some urgent inquiry we were informed that they were all grazing high up on the mountain pastures.

"Let's not bother about a yak," I said. But Mingma sent a couple of big schoolboys rushing up the mountainside, where they were soon lost to view. While all this was happening, Ang Rita had disappeared. Now he was seen returning at the head of a long line of fifty Khumjung boys and girls. He looked like the Pied Piper. Then, from every direction, parents and children came crowding to the chorten. We waited another twenty minutes, searching the hillside in vain.

"We'll have to leave Father Christmas and his yak until later," I said, feeling rather desperate.

"They're coming," one of the children shouted, and everybody looked up toward the hospital, where we could see the bobbing red figure of Father Christmas astride a gigantic black and hairy beast. At first Lois didn't dare look, but the yak proved quite unruffled by the situation and walked down the stony track completely oblivious to the screaming throng of youngsters and the peculiar load on its back. No one in Khumjung or Khunde had ever seen anybody dressed as strangely as Max in his scarlet garb. He arrived at the chorten and was instantly surrounded by two hundred enthralled children. The basket of presents had arrived intact on the back of the yak and when the excitement had calmed down a little, Max started putting gifts in all the outstretched hands. This was the signal for bedlam to be let loose. But the yak either had no nerves in its body or had had a particularly good breakfast that morning, for it never moved or blinked an eyelid. Max threw sweets and gifts all over the place and the children ducked and dived after them in great excitement. One rather retarded Sherpa boy of nineteen took a very firm hold on the basket of gifts and tried to wrench it out of Max's hand, but Max in most un-Father Christmassy fashion gave him a very stiff dig in the ribs, and all continued happily until the last present had been distributed.

"Good-bye, good-bye," called Father Christmas as he and his trusty steed departed peacefully up the path. The crowd answered with a cheerful roar of appreciation. We stood and watched the humorous, waving red figure on its unlikely mount until it disappeared behind the hospital.

"Now for the Maori dancing," I yelled over the din. The dancing troupe formed itself into a straggling line with an admiring and excited audience surrounding it. We rushed through our items at great speed.

"Now for the Sherpa and Nepali dancing," I screamed over the chatter, and our three scholarship boys went into wild action as they pushed and pulled some of the school children out of the crowd and into a row to perform their songs and dances.

"First race!" I called to the three boys, who immediately rushed into the crowd once more and hauled out five medium-sized boys, who had to carry a potato balanced on a spoon held in their mouths. As each new competition or race came along I'd explain in very simple English to the scholarship boys exactly how it was done, and they in turn would translate it into Sherpa for the competitors. We had three-legged races, wheelbarrow races—all the usual party entertainment. The onlookers screamed with laughter at every race and even the dignified Kappa Kalden laughed at the antics of his grandchildren.

I was quite hoarse by the time we got to the final race, which was a paper chase for the tough Sherpa men who had helped build the hospital. A long uphill course had been laid out and we felt that the man who won this race would truly deserve a good prize.

"On your mark, go!" I yelled and they all rushed off at great speed with strong bouncy Pemba Tarkay and Phu Dorje well in the lead. But we hadn't reckoned on the cunning of Ang Tsering who, once he was out of sight, nipped across to the end of the paper trail and came in well and truly first, so creating complete confusion and much laughter. Meanwhile the other Sherpas dashed heroically on, and when they finally flung themselves at the finishing tape, they were so exhausted that they just lay on their backs looking completely winded and limp from their terrific efforts. Who deserved first prize? No one could make up his mind, so we presented each tired competitor with a prize, including the wicked Ang Tsering.

The party seemed to have been a great success with the children and with their parents, who like parents anywhere in the world loved to see their children performing.

They were all beaming with pleasure and quite prepared to stay for many more hours. Rather reluctantly I announced in my now crackling voice, "Finished, everything finished," and we all walked up to the hospital to replenish our strength with a large bowl of soup.

We had been so busy all morning that it was quite a shock to remember that this was our last day in Khunde. Next morning we were to start down valley and walk a hundred miles across Nepal to Jiri, where the Swiss Technical Aid Mission had an agricultural research farm and airfield.

The first person to recover from the children's party was Siku. Ed had just told him that he and Pemba Tarkay would be traveling to India with us as a reward for their faithful service to the Hillary and Pearl families. Because of this Siku wanted to rush back home to his village of Phortse and tell his wife the good news, but he knew that his first duties lay toward the Burrah Memsahib and her children. So at 2 P.M. he carefully filled our hot water bags, popped them inside our beds, and then strode off to see his wife. I am sure it never occurred to him that the bags might get cold before nightfall, but we were very touched by his thoughtfulness. We packed all afternoon. Without Siku to show me where everything was, I wondered seriously if I would ever straighten out our belongings. As well as packing our clothes we had to think of food and the kitchen equipment for the long trek. There were thirteen of us in the party—the Pearls, the Hillarys, the two carpenters, and Mike. Dianne and John McKinnon were staying on at the hospital to continue their medical work for the rest of the year. We had to take stores of butter, sugar, cheese, biscuits, and chocolate, and we planned to buy chicken, rice, and potatoes as we traveled. What hard work all this thinking was! To make concentration even more difficult, we were visited by some of our closest Sherpa friends, who had come to say farewell with the usual offerings of liquid refreshment. Kappa Kalden and his wife and Ang Rita were among them.

"You are another father to my son," said Kappa Kalden with deep solemnity. We felt very honored by his words but it was a great responsibility, and we only hoped that when Ang Rita took up his scholarship in another part of Nepal that no harm would come to him. Kappa Kalden offered us a powerful brew of rakshi which I sipped very gingerly until the family took their leave. After they had gone Ed poured the remainder of his rakshi onto the fire and tongues of blue flame leaped into the air as if we were performing some pagan rite.

CHAPTER 13

Trekking to Solu

....

Early on the morning of our departure from Khunde I was wakened by the industrious Siku who had already returned from his overnight stay at Phortse. We leaped out of bed and breakfasted promptly in the hope of getting away quickly. But as we stepped out of the kitchen we were confronted by almost the entire population of Khunde and Khumjung who had come to say farewell. They had brought ceremonial scarves and many bottles of rakshi. After two hours of constant scarf-giving and sipping of beverages the strain of it all began to take its toll. Most of the children were looking tearful at the thought of their imminent departure, and our porters were getting restless from the delay.

"Cheer up, children," Ed said, "at least you are taking most of your special friends with you." And this was true, for all the Sherpas who had helped us to Base Camp were walking with us to Jiri as well. Dianne and John looked cheerful and carefree at the thought of being on their own among the Sherpas for a year, but we hated to leave them behind. With a hurried wave we departed quickly down the hill. When we arrived at the top of the ridge overlooking Khunde and Khumjung, we stopped to look back for the last time and to say our silent good-byes to the two villages that had come to mean so much to us. I think there were tears in the eyes of most of us.

It was Blackie who cheered us up and started us on the way again. He rushed along in forceful fashion, never noticing the drops in the track. There'd just be a wild scream and we'd see a rolling ball of black fur careering down the slope.

Our scholarship boys accompanied us to Namche and every so often they'd produce a pretty Tibetan rug and spread it out so that we could rest in comfort. We had various social calls in Namche, but we made them brief as we wanted to get to Lukla before dark. We visited the Burrah Hakim and the Chief of Police to say good-bye, then Mingma hurried us on our way.

I found it a long hard walk that day. We covered about fifteen miles and the children gamboled on so far ahead that we completely lost them and so could not stop for lunch until three o'clock, when we finally all met up again. The Hillary children were admonished very firmly by their father and told to stick together at all times when traveling in mountain country. Blackie continued to roll along at great speed, but fell twelve feet down the side of the track, narrowly missing the hungry Dudh Kosi river. Poor Siku had to carry him once more.

It was always fascinating to walk along the more frequented tracks of the Himalayas, for you never knew what interesting sight was waiting for you round the corner. We passed an ancient and very dignified lama who was hobbling along with the help of a stick, followed by his porters and lesser monks. Then we met a cheerful group of Sherpas carrying grain to their village. They were sitting beside the track having a picnic lunch and their little dog took such fright at the sight of us that it dashed wildly back along the path. The woman who owned it had been carrying a seventy-pound load all morning, but she jumped to her feet and chased the dog for nearly a mile. She found it cowering in some bushes, and, looking as fresh as a daisy, she picked it up and ran energetically back to her load.

We were next passed by a long line of Nepalese coolies carrying great bamboo baskets filled with chilies. A little later we came face to face with an elegantly dressed European wandering up the track with a minute pack on his back and a neatly folded umbrella, which he used as a walking stick.

"Is this the main road to Namche?" he inquired of us.

"Yes," we said.

"Thank you," was his only reply as he continued on.

Most colorful of all the travelers was an old Khumjung friend of ours who was leading four handsome black yaks heavily laden with grain. The yaks were obviously his pride and joy, for they were brightly decorated with big tassels around their ears and tails and gay bells around their necks. These sights kept us going until we reached the last long hill before Lukla. Here all our energy seemed to leave us, and tired and thirsty we stopped for a drink from a fresh mountain stream beside a water-driven revolving prayer wheel. At the completion of each revolution the sweet note of a high-toned bell would peel out into the still evening air.

My first thought on arriving in camp was to find Blackie. He was stretched out in front of the fire looking like a little piece of black rag that somebody had flung carelessly on the ground. Mingma decided that Blackie needed special care and attention and he told Ang Dooli very firmly that she was to look after him.

There was soon a great crowd of us bustling around in the dark, for we had not only our faithful Sherpas but also forty porters to carry our trekking equipment and our boxes of "Tibetan treasures." Our porters made an unusual group. There was one of Kappa Kalden's sons, a handsome, delicate, and highly strung fellow of about twenty-three; there was a nun dressed in magenta robes and with closely shaven head who was one of Mingma's relations; the Khunde headman's son was carrying a load too; and we even had half a dozen of the thyroid-deficient Sherpas, who were a jolly but rather brainless lot. As camp followers we had various friends and relations of these people who had taken the opportunity to accompany us for a pleasant excursion.

To add to the holiday atmosphere of this journey the British Ambassador, Mr. Arthur Kellas, his wife, and three children were planning to fly into Lukla the following day and join us for the trek out. This would swell our numbers for the trek to eighteen, nine of whom were children.

All campers remember with nostalgia the pleasant evenings spent around a warm fire with the clouds swirling above and a cup of hot tea in hand. It sounds very well in theory, but every now and then it doesn't work out in practice. The night was rather cold so I sat on a rock quite close to the warm fire. After a while the hard rock became so painful that I was forced to seek a softer seat on the ground. Half an hour later I realized that the uneven sloping ground was causing me to fall over backward every time I relaxed, so I moved again. Now the fickle wind changed and the smoke came straight into my eyes. The delights of Himalayan travel seemed to evade me that night, but such minor irritations are part and parcel of camping life and one soon forgets them.

When we poked our noses gingerly out of the tents next day, the whole camp seemed to be lost in damp weeping clouds. It had snowed a little during the night, leaving a white blanket of depression over the whole scene. There was very little chance of our friends flying to Lukla in this weather, so Ed told the Sherpas to leave the tents up. We stood around in the cold mists waiting for the weather to clear. As if to tease us, the wind started blowing away the clouds and we were soon bathed in warm sunshine, although down toward Katmandu it looked as bad as ever. It was decided that we would make it a rest day, so we basked in the sun and did nothing, very pleasantly. The only break in this peaceful monotony was a visit from the local village council. They also needed a new roof for their village temple, and plied us with the usual long speeches of praise and several bottles of strong drink.

I thoroughly enjoyed the day of inactivity, reading an entire book and going for a short walk to visit some of the houses near the airfield. Here we discovered an industrious little band of Sherpas packing a strange root into large baskets, which they then carefully covered with a bamboo lid. The root was so precious that the owners were willing to have six baskets of it flown to Katmandu at considerable cost. We tried to find out what the merchandise was. At first they seemed a little secretive and embarrassed and we immediately thought that it must be some illegal drug like opium, but after a great deal of questioning we extracted the information that the root was sold in India for use in making a cough mixture. We smelled and tasted it but ended up just as mystified as when we started.

That night the weather closed right in and we weren't very optimistic about the Kellases making a landing the next day. Ahead of us was a trek of at least a hundred miles and if we didn't make a start we would not have time to complete all our plans. So it was decided that we would leave the very efficient and upright Tenzing Niendra to wait for them at Lukla, and that we would continue on.

He was left with food, camping gear, and various plans covering all contingencies, and we only hoped that everything would work out successfully.

The weather was terrible when we finally left Lukla. A soft drizzle of snow and rain made the path very slippery and thick mists played around us in ghostly fashion. Blackie was in form and rushed ahead of the children, leading them down a steep hillside in helter-skelter fashion. We could hear them ahead of us in the mist and only hoped they were keeping to the right track. We caught up to them at the little village of Surkya, which four years before had seen the start of a tragic period in the Khumbu. A porter coming from Katmandu had arrived in this village with smallpox and a terrible epidemic swept through the area. Ed had been school-building at the time and arranged to have smallpox vaccine flown in as quickly as possible, but at least twenty-five people died and many were left terribly scarred for life.

Above Surkya the track climbed a very steep hillside, whose summit was lost in the clouds. We struggled upward for many hours through gaunt dark and dripping forests, and soon became breathless and disillusioned, for we had been told that the walk down valley would be easy after Everest Base Camp. In a little clearing in the forest we lit a fire and had an early lunch to give us the strength to continue. We enjoyed cabin biscuits and canned salmon and Blackie was allowed to lick out the empty tins. Once or twice the clouds lifted for a fleeting moment and we had glorious and slightly ethereal views of dark, lichen-covered forests plunging down to the depths of the Dudh Kosi valley. We heard the buzzing of aircraft engines far above us on two occasions but knew there was no chance of a successful landing.

Up . . . up . . . I decided this mountain was truly never-

Phudorje, with a little volunteer work from Peter, cooks a dish that has them dubious—but shouldn't. It is—or will be—potato chips.

Father Christmas—Max Pearl—hands out presents to a waiting world. He is seated on a yak.

The walking party crosses the Lamdura Banyang Pass.

Belinda Hillary with Blackie.

Tensing (right), who was with Hillary on Everest, and his lovely wife, Daku.

Sarah Hillary beams her pleasure at her new Sherpa clothing.

ending. We dragged ourselves over slippery stones and snowy paths. It would have been such a help if the clouds had cleared enough for us to have seen where we were going. The mosses and the lichens on this great forested hillside were quite fascinating and we collected bunches of them. Why we did this I don't know, but all humans seem to have an acquisitive instinct and it gave us pleasure to gather such a variety of dainty fronds from the sides of the track. There were also pieces of sparkling mica and little bushes covered with red berries, which Sarah collected and made into a surprisingly attractive necklace.

With one final lunge of energy we gained the pass and rested beside a sheltering prayer wall. The sweet scent of starry white and pink daphne flowers filled the air, but it was too cold to sit around.

"Just imagine the poor Kellases having to walk up this path on their first day of trekking," I said to Ed. "How on earth will they manage it?" It certainly was a grim thought and we felt very sorry for them.

Chilled from our brief halt, we followed the track across the mountain slopes high above the valley. We scrambled across rock faces and brushed past delicate fronds of rain-soaked bamboo. Then the track dropped suddenly below the clouds, down and down for many hundreds of feet, until with intense relief we saw the welcoming flames of a fire on a delightful grassy ledge in the forest. We pushed through the last few dripping rhododendrons to our camp, where Phu Dorje was dragging a giant tree out of the forest for firewood. It seemed impossible that he could move such a load unaided, and, not satisfied with this great effort, he returned and brought out three long heavy boughs for seats around the cosy fire. We spent most of the evening backing away from its ever-increasing flames, but we dried all our clothes and the Sherpas celebrated the occasion by actually washing the tea towels and hanging them beside us.

It was so comfortable beside the fire that we stayed up until the very late hour of nine o'clock. All night the snow pattered gently on the roofs of our tents and by morning I was wondering whether we would ever be blessed with another fine day. Normally Ang Passang and Nima would light the fire and make the early cup of tea, but at daylight they were still lying cosily in their sleeping bags and brave Ang Tsering did the job—wearing a bright knitted cap given him by Belinda the day before, and with a clean tea towel nonchalantly tossed over his shoulder.

It was much too damp and cold for breakfast in this shady spot, so we romped down the mountain toward warmer temperatures. Soon the sun came out and, joy of joys, we saw a few bright scarlet rhododendron blossoms. The slope was never-ending, but at least we were going downhill. There were many murmurs of "When is breakfast?" and "Can we have some chocolate?" from the young members of the party, but we had decided not to stop for a meal until we reached the Dudh Kosi river. Mingma must have heard the hungry remarks, for he disappeared into a house and returned quite soon with a bag full of freshly cooked popcorn. It was absolutely delicious, even though Sherpa popcorn doesn't pop as thoroughly as ours. We munched our way downhill, feeling very cheerful and well looked after. In the Rai village of Jubing, Mingma bought fifty oranges at a price of one rupee for thirty. We reached the wild waters of the Dudh Kosi and had our long-awaited picnic brunch in a glorious grassy spot among the boulders. We were now down to six thousand feet and the temperatures were so mild that we seemed to have left winter far behind. To add to our enjoyment, the plane flew high above us toward Lukla and there wasn't a cloud in the sky, so we knew the Kellases would be able to land.

For an hour we walked through tall subtropical forest. Small orchid plants covered the mossy tree trunks and rocks, and I gathered some of these to take home, as I liked the thought of a little bit of the Himalayas growing in my own garden. The scenery changed. We climbed out of the valley and onto terraced slopes dotted with neat Nepali farm houses. Higher and higher we climbed, up airy ridges with wide mountain views, until we left the arable land behind and were once more in pine and rhododendron forest. It was like fairyland with dainty half-frozen streams dashing down stony valleys and graceful waving bamboos clustered beneath tall gnarled trees. Through this lovely foreground we caught glimpses of towering mountains, while all around us the little daphne bushes carpeted the forest floor with starlike blossoms. We picked bunches of the flowers and inhaled their perfume.

Our camp site was a wide clearing chiseled out of the steep valley wall. It was a magnificent position and could hardly have been more beautiful or spectacular. We celebrated New Year's Eve around a large fire, watching the deep shadows engulfing the Dudh Kosi valley below, while the mountains glowed in the last rays of a brilliant pink sunset.

Tragedy is never too far away in Nepal. A Sherpa came into camp seeking medical aid. On his back in a bamboo basket was a twelve-year-old lad, weak and pale. Max and Mike examined him and diagnosed a serious kidney condition, plus extreme anemia. The boy was very close to death. Only blood transfusions and hospital care could save his life. Since the nearest clinic was three days' walk away, and it was the only hope, we hired a porter to help carry the boy and then sent the family off on a desperate race over the mountain ridges to try and reach hospital in time. The boy's calm, patient eyes seemed to know that the race was already lost and we were saddened by the thought that for weeks he had been within a day's walk of our hospital at Khumjung and his father hadn't known enough to bring him in.

To add to the drama of the evening, Mingma arrived in camp with a huge load on his back. We managed to prise the story out of him. Pema, the artist's son, had imbibed too freely of local beer and had fallen asleep on the track beside his load. Mingma had been unable to wake him, so he added the sixty-five pounds to his own thirty pounds and carried this huge load up the last thousand feet into camp. Pema stumbled into camp later in the evening, filled with shame and remorse. He was told he had been sacked. With a woebegone look on his face, he made his own little fire nearby, obviously hoping that the Burrah Sahib and Mingma would relent in the morning.

We were wakened in the morning by the noise of our tents being pulled down around us. We hurriedly dressed and dived for the warmth of the fire, where tea and biscuits were ready. The day was quite brilliant and our senses soared with the joy of it all. We wandered up through fir trees and rhododendrons, sniffing the scent of daphne flowers in the crisp morning air. Soon we were up in the snow again, and the trees were white and Christmassy. The track had been pounded into solid ice and it was hard to concentrate on one's feet and the glorious views at the same time. Shafts of sunlight probed the forest and snow crystals sparkled, while the mountains echoed with songs from our happy Sherpas. We felt completely disassociated from the mundane world.

Toward the top of the hill the singing was drowned by the wild roaring of the wind sweeping over the pass. We battled our way over the summit and out of the worst of the wind and then found a sea of soft white clouds billowing toward us like great ocean waves. We plunged down into it and for many hours wandered through weird forests with drifting mists and occasional, watery sunlight.

With breath-taking abruptness we rounded a bend in the path and found ourselves once more under the blue sky, with all the clouds behind us. A short climb brought us to the crest of another great ridge with a new series of valleys below us. It was such a sudden change that we all let out wild cries of excitement and stopped for a moment to absorb the immense new landscape. There were clusters of prayer flags whistling and waving in the wind and Mingma told us that this was where our track divided. One path went straight down toward the valley and the prosperous Sherpa village of Paphlu, and the other track went along the ridge to the Swiss Aid Center of Jalsa. We were all particularly keen to see Jalsa, as it is a large resettlement project for Tibetan refugees, with carpetmaking as the major industry.

"It is not very far to Jalsa," said Mingma. So off we went, leaving the porters to go down to Paphlu to make camp. The track was straight and level, but it went on and on. Even the bouncy children became disheartened. Belinda had her hand taken by a determined Ang Dooli, who literally pulled her for the rest of the day. They looked so funny walking together, for Ang Dooli was very short, even for a Sherpa, and Belinda was quite tall for her age. Ang Dooli swept Belinda along at such speed that we soon lost sight of them.

It was late afternoon and very cold when we reached

the Aid Center, which proved to be a self-help type of organization with a Swiss director and his wife and a Tibetan refugee staff. The Swiss had installed the Tibetans in attractive but simple houses and most of the residents worked in the factory. There were schools for the children. The refugees were organized into a tight little community under a cooperative scheme. We recognized many of our trader friends who had visited us in Khunde and had a happy reunion.

The carpet factory was about to close for the night, so we made a hurried visit and were most impressed by the standard of work. Traditional Tibetan designs were being followed by the carpetmakers, who chanted the pattern changes as they worked. The finest Swiss chemical dyes were used for coloring. The Jalsa factory was finding a ready market for its carpets, most of them being exported to Europe and a few being sold in Katmandu.

For some time I had been thinking how much I'd enjoy a cup of tea before setting off on the walk to Paphlu, and as if in answer to my thoughts we were invited to a little Tibetan teahouse in the middle of the settlement. It was warm and cosy inside. We drank glasses and glasses of hot tea with great enjoyment and there were cries of delight when three plates of biscuits were offered us. To my disappointment the food disappeared so quickly that I didn't have time to eat anything myself and it was also a little embarrassing, as biscuits were hard to obtain in Jalsa. Sarah's pockets were bulging unnaturally. I realized that she must have stuffed in about half a dozen biscuits, which wasn't surprising, as it was a very long time since breakfast.

When we left the village we were farewelled by nearly all its inhabitants.

Paphlu is situated in the great valley system of Solu. It is a beautiful and thriving place with fertile pastures and patches of rich pine forest. The Sherpas who settled in Paphlu many generations before had become wealthy landowners, with large and opulent houses, and they lived in feudal splendor. Concealed by the darkness, we hurried past their impressive gates like the poorest of country cousins. We found our camp on a flat sheltered field surrounded by tall fir trees, and Nima escorted us to our tents with his flashlight. We were all glad to crawl into our sleeping bags after a hasty meal.

The next day was to be an important one. Ed had arranged to be in the village of Junbesi, ten miles away, by 3 P.M. for talks with the local school committee. Also, we wanted to visit the famous Buddhist monastery of Chewong. An early start was essential. The only problem was Belinda. Her gym shoes were completely worn out and it was imperative that we get them replaced in the district bazaar at the village of Seluri. Mingma assured us he would do the necessary purchasing and be back in time for breakfast.

At 5 A.M. it was still dark when Mingma left on his hunt for the shoes. Unbeknown to us, an energetic Max had accompanied him. Breakfast was cooked and eaten, tents dismantled, and loads made up and still there was no sign of the pair. We were about to leave without them when two very dignified Sherpa officials came riding into camp. They were from Seluri, the Government headquarters of Solu district, and wanted us to pay the town an official visit. To their great disappointment we explained that time would not permit. They also wanted advice about a new airstrip they were building in the area, as they knew of Ed's success with the Lukla airfield. I offered our guests coffee and food while they talked long and earnestly about the various projects they were undertaking and their progressive ideas for Solu.

Two hours after we should have departed for Chewong, Max and Mingma finally came in sight. Mingma was tired but victorious. He had found no shoes in Seluri and had pushed on down the valley for two or three more miles to the town of Dorpu, where he had at last discovered a pair of bright red gym shoes for Belinda and an equally handsome pair of white ones for Sarah. But that was not all. Clutched in Max's hand was a little parcel, which he quickly unwrapped to show, with beaming face, that he had bought an exquisite Buddha image. There was a low moan from his family. Max quickly told them the price, which, though fairly high, was not as disastrous as they had expected.

"Well, I'm sorry," said Ed. "You can all go to Chewong, but Max and I will have to go straight to Junbesi. There's no time left."

"No, you can't do that," I said. "We might never be here again." After a lot of talk we finally persuaded the two men to accompany us.

"But you'll have to go very quickly," they cautioned.

High above us like a jewel set into the wall of the valley was the famous monastery of Chewong, respected by all Sherpas and Tibetans. We approached it by a narrow zigzag track up steep bluffs. The buildings looked perfect in their setting and the view was breath-taking—not the usual view of Himalayan peaks but a much more peaceful outlook. The deep Solu valley with its patchwork of farms and villages was spread out far below and seemed to sleep in the midday sun. The hills decreased in height to the south, where they gradually blended into the hot plains of India. The lamas' houses were decorated with bright window boxes. Tall fir trees leaned over the buildings as if to protect them from the precipice below.

Inside the temple was an open courtyard, with walls magnificently painted in a series of handsome but terrifying dragons measuring up to twenty feet long. Two or three large black mastiffs came and watched us as we stood in admiring silence, so the children held Blackie very carefully. The monks had agreed to do a Puja for us. We walked into the inky darkness of the main temple, where they told us to be seated around the sides of the imposing but gloomy room. For the next quarter of an hour we were wafted into a strange, medieval world of musky incense and the chanting of prayers. Every now and then the intoning was interrupted by Himalayan trumpets, drums, and oboes, whose eerie music shattered the stillness like thunder. Terrified, Blackie burrowed deeply into my down jacket. When the Puja was finished the senior monk invited us into the monastery kitchen for glasses of hot sweet tea. We sat in comfort round a charcoal brazier dreading the thought of our long walk to Junbesi.

"Tuchi, tuchiche," (Thank you, thank you very much) we said in our best Sherpa and made our departure. As we stood outside the main door, blinking in the sunlight, a giant lammergeier with mighty outstretched wings floated above us. It looked us over in scornful fashion and then drifted away on the wind with contemptuous ease, until our straining eyes could no longer see it in the fierce blue of the midday sky. We earth-bound creatures watched with envy and then rushed off down the steep rocky path toward Junbesi.

CHAPTER 14

Village of the Moon

....

Everyone was walking much too fast. I hate going quickly, and thumping downhill almost jars me into little pieces. Besides, it seemed sacrilegious to travel at such speed through this lovely countryside. The faithful Siku kept behind me so that I would not be lost or forgotten. When we reached the valley floor, there were wide flats beside the river, and I sped across these in an attempt to show the party I wasn't so weak after all. On each side of us, steep grassy hillsides stretched up abruptly.

"Magnificent sheep country," Ed muttered. But we could see only a handful of miserable Tibetan sheep and a few yaks grazing on the dry winter grass. We all agreed that New Zealand sheep from the mountains of the South Island would be ideally suited for this area.

We pounded through the country like a desperate army with no time to rest or enjoy the beauties around us. At last we could see the village across the river ahead. It nestled in a sheltered and luxuriant corner of the valley, with a neat group of whitewashed houses reflecting the afternoon sun. It was easy to understand why the local people had called this place Junbesi, the Village of the Moon.

We were late for our appointment and we were concerned that the school committee might have stopped waiting for us, but our fears proved groundless. Half a mile outside the village we were brought to a standstill by the entire school population of Junbesi. A hundred and twenty children were there, all dressed in their very best clothes, with clean shining faces, and tidy hair decorated with bright ribbons. Two of the boys in the forefront of the group held a large banner saying "Wel-come" and two other boys were leading Tibetan ponies with bells around their necks and gay Tibetan rugs over the wooden saddles. The smiling-faced young schoolmaster and his assistant explained to us that the children were here to escort us to the village. Ed and I very hastily turned down the offer of a ride on a pony and suggested the children would enjoy it. So off they went, having turn and turn about while we remained behind to be welcomed. Each child had brought a ceremonial scarf and that made a hundred and twenty scarves. To make things more complicated I already had a camera in one hand and Ang Tsering's ski stick in the other. Ed received most of the ceremonial scarves, but I was given at least forty. I tried to take pictures of the children as they came to honor us but got more and more mixed up in my ski stick. The scarves started to fall off or thread themselves around my camera and I found it difficult to concentrate on the welcoming ceremony.

"Can't you control your belongings?" Ed asked a little testily, for I seemed to be getting more and more muddled every minute. When the last scarf had been offered, we were led by the teachers toward the village. As I walked I shed ceremonial scarves to the right and left in regal style and the little children picked them up and handed them back to me with the utmost patience.

This had been only a foretaste of our welcome to Junbesi. As we approached the school grounds we could see that just about every villager was standing there ready to greet us. There were more "Wel-come" signs over the gateway and we were ushered into the schoolroom, where already many people were seated. Our hosts led us to comfortable chairs and offered us a large bowl of oranges and bananas. As usual I was embarrassed by the speed with which these disappeared. You would have thought we had six starving children with us, as their appetites seemed quite uncontrollable.

Ang Dorji, the chairman of the school committee, presided over the meeting. First he introduced the prize-winners of the previous year and then all the senior pupils were brought forward. There was an impressive number for a school that had only been in existence for about three years.

"We have over a hundred and twenty pupils attending the school and, as you can see, this one-roomed building is not big enough. Also, Burrah Sahib, we need another teacher to cope with these great numbers," said Ang Dorji. We were thrilled to see how the school had developed, but it was quite apparent that something would have to be done.

Ed rose to his feet and made a speech of appreciation to the committee and parents, and then told them he couldn't make a decision until the evening.

"I must work out my finances," he explained.

"There are refreshments ready in the Gompa courtyard," said Ang Dorji, "and the village would like to entertain you tonight. You will all be sleeping in the Gompa or in an adjacent house." It sounded quite delightful. We were only too happy to agree with his arrangements.

The village of Junbesi is a sophisticated and worldly

place, for many of the Sherpas, as in Paphlu, are comparatively wealthy people. They live closer to Katmandu,
for one thing, and a few of their richer sons have been
sent there for their education. Many of them speak a little
English and dress in the Nepali fashion rather than in
the Sherpa mode. In fact, Junbesi is a rather successful
bridge between the Nepali and Sherpa cultures.

Up at the Gompa one of the balconies overlooking the
courtyard had been turned into a refreshment area. We
were given Tibetan tea and tasty twisted rice cakes
covered with sugar. As soon as we had gulped a little of
the tea, the cups were whisked away and filled with rakshi.
It was a good brew and we almost enjoyed it as we con-
versed with our hosts. All our children had vanished into
thin air, but we had no fears for them in this friendly spot.
I was brought temporarily down to earth when Belinda
appeared on the scene saying that she needed a toilet
urgently.

"Take one of the bigger girls," I said, "and she will help
you find a secluded spot. We are too busy to worry about
such things now." We relaxed once more, but only for a
minute or two, for one of our Sherpas came rushing in
breathlessly to inform us that the Ambassador Sahib was
approaching. The whole village was turned into a frenzy,
for they had never had so many foreign VIPs in their midst
before. The rice cakes and the rakshi were completely forgotten as we rose in a body and dashed out of the temple
courtyard and down the steps toward the big village
chorten. After standing in the cold for two or three minutes, we realized this was another example of a sharp-
eyed Sherpa spying our friends two or three miles away,
so we returned to the comforts of the Gompa. Soon
after, a chagrined Belinda arrived to announce that the
worst had happened. She hadn't been able to find her way

out of the village and was in the process of freezing solid. We had completely lost sight of Siku—who had been carrying Blackie and my camera—and all our belongings, but Mingma told me I could find all these things in a big Sherpa house at the side of the Gompa. I hurried around the Gompa with Belinda and soon spied the house, but to get to it we had to walk down a narrow little stone alley, at the end of which two wicked-looking Apso dogs were barking fiercely. We retraced our steps and approached the house from another direction. When we finally arrived, there was Siku pumping up air mattresses and making a nice little home for us. I found some dry clothes for my shivering daughter but could find no private place for her to change in.

"Other room?" I inquired in my best Nepali.

Siku proudly led me to a tiny room at the end of the passage, complete with door and large lock. There were a couple of dainty-looking holes in the floor, and I realized it was the household toilet. We closed the door firmly. While Belinda changed I explored my surroundings. Below was a barn inhabited by a dozen peaceful yaks. I only hoped they wouldn't mind when the toilet facilities were put to use.

We hurried back to the Gompa in time to rush out once more and meet the Kellas family, who were marching up the hill toward us at a very energetic pace. They were wielding handsome walking sticks and they looked fresh and surprisingly clean after their vigorous march to catch up with us. By taking a more direct route they had saved a day of walking, but even so it had been a long journey and we were most impressed with their strength and endurance. The Kellas family consisted of Arthur and Bridget and their three children, Miranda, aged thirteen, Ian, eleven, and Roger, nine. Peter eyed the boys with undisguised relief, and Miranda immediately made friends with Lynn and Ann.

As a further test of their stamina they were now embroiled in overwhelming Sherpa hospitality. Junbesi is at ten thousand feet and with the departure of the sun the temperature dropped very sharply. We were glad to crowd around a large fire in the middle of the courtyard and thaw our frozen fingers and toes. Chairs and tables were brought to make us more comfortable. When it became dark, a couple of pressure lamps—minus glass—were put on the table to flare in a most sensational manner every few minutes. Dinner soon appeared, with piles of boiled rice and some rather ancient yak meat that had been fried for a considerable length of time. We were also served a delicious onion omelette, and when we had eaten all we could possibly hold, fresh oranges were placed on the tables. All the Junbesi residents stood around the courtyard watching us eat and drink. It was a real village affair and everyone took a great interest and pride in the proceedings.

After dinner two young American anthropologists joined us by the fire. They were spending a year in the village doing a thesis for their doctorates and seemed to have fitted very smoothly into the community. With the help of their guitar we soon embarked on a noisy singsong that carried on so happily and lustily that the program arranged by the village committee for our enjoyment was nearly forgotten. Fortunately someone noticed a shivering dancer lurking in a dark corner so we hastily called the meeting to order.

To start the official program we had more speeches, and the most eagerly awaited one was the Burrah Sahib's. Ed had been scribbling figures on a piece of grubby paper to see if the annual grant he received from World Book Encyclopedia to run the schools could be stretched a little further.

"I have worked out my finances," he announced to a hushed audience, "and I am pleased to tell you that there will be enough money to enlarge the Junbesi school and give you another teacher." There was a hum of pleasure, which stopped when Ed continued. "But you will be expected to supply free labor for the building, to carry all the rock and timber, and to give free accommodation to the teacher."

The school committee nodded their agreement and smiled their great satisfaction while Ang Dorji thanked Ed on behalf of the village.

"And now we will have the dancing," he concluded.

For the next two hours we stood around the blazing fire and watched a mixture of gay Nepali dancing and dignified Sherpa and Tibetan traditional dancing. The school teacher and his assistant performed the Nepali dancing, and everyone joined in the singing of the folk songs that accompanied it. Their cheerful uninhibited style was very attractive, but the most popular items of the evening were the Tibetan dances, performed by six pretty Sherpa girls dressed in colorful blouses and tunics, and brightly striped aprons. They were delightfully shy and collapsed in fits of delicate schoolgirl giggles whenever they forgot a word or action. Their natural charm, healthy rosy cheeks, and sleek shining black pigtails tied with gay ribbons completely bewitched the audience. To add to the enchantment, the lamps flickered so violently that at times the dancers would be lost in the inky gloom only to reappear startlingly in a flare of light.

It was about half past ten when we decided that the young members of the party must definitely get some sleep. We thanked Ang Dorji profusely for the hospitality and although he was prepared to go on with the entertainment all night, he loudly announced the end of the festivities. Holding a highly dangerous pressure lamp, he led us carefully to the back of the Gompa, keeping to the left in good Sherpa Buddhist fashion. It made the journey back to our sleeping quarters twice as long, but as Ang Dorji said, "Much more lucky."

Siku was there to welcome us, and on the door someone had written in our honor "Guest room" in rather shaky letters. There was a small shelf on one of the walls with "Wel-come" written on it, and above this Siku had put an empty Beaujolais wine can with a candle in it, lighting the room in most artistic and bistro-like manner. A huge wooden bedstead took up half the room. On it he had placed the air mattresses and sleeping bags of the children. The parents had been relegated to the floor, but in all our sleeping bags were hot water bottles so we felt very well treated. Sleeping in tents at these altitudes was rather cold, and I hoped that this night inside a house would be quite a lot warmer and that we'd sleep better as a result. I was to be disappointed, however, for down below a large noisy family was making a surprising lot of disturbance. One member of the family must have overimbibed a little, for he kept singing the first two phrases and a half of "Shenandoah." He sang it over and over. How he learned the song and who he was I will never know, but the maddening monotony of it sounded like a needle stuck in a record groove. All night long a baby cried, and every so often the mother would give him a resounding slap and he would wail in a pathetic decrescendo, ending in a quivering whimper. By morning I likened the night to my sleepless one at Lake Camp. Siku came in carrying mugs of tea, but the tea had traveled so far from the Gompa kitchen that it was stone cold. My only hope was that breakfast would revive me, so I jumped quickly out of my bag and hurried to the courtyard.

Breakfast time was spent in viewing the interior of the Gompa, which, even though old and dilapidated, had some magnificent treasures. A superbly painted Buddha on the main lower floor was so large that it stretched through to the ceiling of the next floor. Upstairs beside the head of the Buddha was a valuable collection of religious books. Ang Dorji, seeing my interest in the old building, invited us to his house, where there were the remains of the oldest known Sherpa building in Solu Khumbu.

"It's just behind the Gompa," he said. "It will only take five minutes." So after a halfhearted attempt to eat cold porridge and potatoes we climbed about five hundred feet up the mountainside and arrived in breathless condition outside Ang Dorji's handsome house. In front was a large and beautifully paved yard with high stone walls to protect it from the winds. On the left was the family temple, at least a hundred years old, its door carefully secured with a huge unwieldy Tibetan padlock. Ang Dorji unlocked this and led us into the main room of the Gompa. The whole place was dark and musty but crammed with old Buddhist relics. There were great collections of religious books tucked away tidily in individual niches around the walls and a magnificent altar crowded with graceful images. One image, we were told, was well over two thousand years old—in fact, made before the time of the Buddha. There was no way to find out if this was true but it was a terribly exciting thought. We were then taken to view the ruins of the two-hundred-year-old house, the first known Sherpa building, which was a rather pathetic collection of stone walls. Then up to the comforts of Ang Dorji's living room in his main house, where we were given cups of tea and watched the youngest Ang

Dorji, aged six, running round the room and kicking a
scrawny dog every time it sat down. No one seemed to
worry about the poor dog's feelings, so we shifted our interest to the small family Gompa in the next room. This
was a charming place with a large glass window which let
in the warm sun. As most Gompas are dark and cold, this
was an unusual break with tradition. All the walls and
shelves were covered with fine paintings and handsome
religious objects. Included in the family treasures was a
large collection of porcelain tea dishes with silver stands.
Ang Dorji led us to comfortable benches covered with
colorful Tibetan rugs and then showed us the greatest
family treasure of all. It was an image of the Buddha
which was so holy and revered that the family only took it
from its silken wrappings once a year.

Our departure from Junbesi gave cause for the presentation of many more ceremonial scarves and many assurances
of appreciation and friendship. We then said our final
good-byes and headed up the hill toward the Lamjura
Banyang pass at just over twelve thousand feet. We had
more than two thousand feet to climb and Belinda complicated matters by saying she had a very sore leg. Max
examined it and came to the conclusion she had pulled a
tendon when riding the horse the day before.

I was most interested to see my daughter's leg while
Max was strapping it up. Instead of her customary nicely
rounded limb, it was now bony and athletic and the skin
was ingrained with Himalayan dust and smoke. Belinda
had lost quite a bit of weight and I immediately began to
feel very maternal and worried, even though I am sure
there wasn't a healthier child anywhere.

The Kellas family proved to be excellent walkers. It was
fun to have some new people accompanying us, for we
had become so used to one another's company that on

the march, we hardly bothered to converse at all. Now we started to chat once more and the long climb seemed to pass much more quickly. Up in the forest there were snowdrifts and a bitter whistling wind and no one suggested a rest until we reached the summit. Then we were so warm from exertion that there was time for me to open a gift sent via the Kellases from Miss Laise, the American Ambassador. It was a box of candy sent as a thank-you present for her visit to the Khumjung hospital. Inside the parcel were twenty-four little packets of caramels and as there were twenty-four of us, families and Sherpas, her choice was most satisfactory.

From the Lamjura Banyang we wandered across the vast snowy uplands—cold and desolate but with a wild beauty—before plunging down into the forest and leaving the snow behind. It was hours since we had eaten and then only the lightest of breakfasts, so everyone was clamoring for food.

"What have you got for us, Ang Tsering?" we said. He looked a little doubtful, so we opened the small box that was meant to contain our lunch. In it were three small week-old Katmandu loaves, half a pound of butter, two cans of sardines, and a jar of honey for eighteen people. Everyone tried to be heroic and not eat too much and by the time we had finished the lucky ones had managed to get a couple of small slices of bread for themselves and perhaps two sardines.

"Well, it's one way of keeping thin," I suggested as I picked up the tail of a sardine that someone had left in the can. The meal had only whetted our appetites on this freezing misty day and I wondered if this would be one of the few occasions in the lives of our children when they would experience real hunger.

The children had become very interested in the woven

bamboo carrying baskets that the Nepalese use with a headband to carry heavy loads around the country. Mingma promised the children he would have some made, so great was the excitement when Ang Dawa, Pemba Tarkay, and Phu Dorje slashed large bundles of small-diameter bamboos and tied them on top of their packs.

The journey down the ridge from the Lamjura Banyang was a trekker's nightmare. The path descended relentlessly for six thousand feet and after stumbling down three thousand feet of it we stopped for the night at the small Seti Gompa. It was a tiny place with only one monk in residence. We made our cooking quarters in a little sheltered courtyard, which had in the center a tall pole with a very long prayer flag attached to it. In his usual down-to-earth fashion, Mingma quickly wrapped the prayer flag around the pole so that it wouldn't get burned, and built a large fire beside it to keep us warm. Now that we were relaxed and comfortable one of the Junbesi men who had accompanied us presented Ed with a bottle of rakshi and a box containing oranges and eggs. We adults spent a pleasant evening pretending to drink rakshi while Mingma took the oranges and handed them to our undernourished children. These same children spent the evening aiding and abetting Ang Dawa with his basketmaking and playing underneath two very large bamboo baskets—pretending they were caged lions. We ate chicken curry and rice round the cosy fire and finished off the evening with more singing. Our sole audience consisted of the lonely monk of Seti, who sat on a small balcony above us and looked rather disapprovingly down upon the cheerful gathering. Just as we were about to go to bed he came downstairs with an attractive copper incense burner and offered it to us for sale. I am ashamed to say that once again the Hillarys were the lucky buyers.

There was quite a sense of urgency about our early-morning getaway, as we knew that the first reasonably warm mountain torrent for washing was only three thousand feet below us. The path was uncomfortably steep and very dusty and we slipped and fell most of the way down in our hurry to reach the river.

By the time we reached the river at six thousand feet the air temperature was delightfully warm, although Ed grimaced with pain when he put his hand in the water. Ang Dooli had already started to wash Belinda's jacket. I handed a large pile of the family clothes to Siku, but I didn't have the heart to ask him to wash Sarah's jacket or mine. I found myself a large cake of soap and squatted in oriental fashion beside the rushing water. The jackets were so dirty that they wouldn't absorb the moisture and floated rather like disembodied spirits on the surface. They floated so well that one of them slipped from my hand and started disappearing down valley toward India. After a hectic but successful scramble to retrieve it, I started rubbing soap violently into the material and then immersed the jacket once more. This time I had a little more success, but my hands were getting very cold and painful. I felt that I couldn't give in with all the tough hard-working Sherpas looking on, and after the first five minutes my hands lost all feeling. It took me a full half hour of soaping, rinsing, rubbing, and slapping on a stone before most of the dirt disappeared. Then I started on the second jacket. After completing half the work my hands, for some strange reason, came back to life and the resulting sensation was so unpleasant that I asked Siku, with his tough and horny hands, to complete the job.

It took two hours before all the clothes were washed and spread out on the sundrenched rocks and shrubs. For another hour we lay in the sun and ate chapatties and fried potatoes for breakfast, knowing full well that sooner or later we would have to wash in the river ourselves. First the Kellas family went off to wash and returned quite soon with shining complexions, drenched hair, and a victorious expression on their faces. They had found a nice big pool and all five of them had been swimming. Their spartan behavior shamed us into resolving to do the same. The Hillarys then departed with a flourish, complete with soap, clean clothes, and toothbrushes. We found what seemed a fairly secluded pool and I managed with a great deal of shouting and blustering to make the children put at least their feet into the water and wash their faces, hands, and hair. The hair washing was a most painful process, and we felt as though our brains were freezing.

My family had shown so little of the pioneering spirit that I decided to have a proper swim to prove that at least one member of the family was not too cowardly. I was undressing for this purpose when Ed drily brought to my attention the fact that the entire population of the valley was now sitting among the bushes on the other side of the stream and watching us with the greatest of interest.

When all the families were reunited, the awful truth came out—only the Kellases had shown sufficient strength of mind to have a complete bath. As if to emphasize their love of cold water, Roger Kellas then fell into the stream and had to wear his mother's woolen sweater as a pair of trousers for the next few hours.

Our cleaning-up operation had taken a long time. It was now midday and time to move. Siku and Pemba Tarkay turned their rucksacks into clotheslines by hanging sticks out of the pockets and draping the washing all over them. They flapped down the track looking like a new breed of giant bird. It had been a most successful morning, and Siku in his usual overindustrious way had washed all our towels before we had time to use them to dry ourselves.

A great change had taken place in the countryside with our descent from the Lamjura Banyang. Well behind us were the Sherpas and the alpine vegetation. Rhododendrons and fir trees had been replaced by thorny bushes and large-leaf subtropical trees, while the local people were true Nepalis living in neat thatched houses surrounded by tidy rice paddies. For two hours we walked through this unaccustomed environment and then started climbing steeply out of the valley toward a distant ridge. We were wet with sticky perspiration by the time we emerged in a hanging valley, grass-covered and golden. There was another small Sherpa community here and on the slopes above were rhododendrons and daphne bushes. We felt completely at home.

Our tents were erected near a small building that housed an old Sherpa prayer wheel, and in front of us, outlined against the sky, were two large white chortens. During the evening, baskets were completed for the six Pearl and Hillary children and the remaining bamboo was used on a small basket for Roger. Great was the excitement among the children, but no one seemed to know how to make a headband for the baskets. Mingma as usual had the right idea. He selected seven strong ceremonial scarves from among our collection and these made very satisfactory headbands.

The standard of living had risen since the arrival of the Kellases and we finished our meal with canned Gruyère, large slices of Christmas cake, and candy. Revitalized by the good food, the children started playing a wild game of tiggy in the dark among the rows of orderly mani walls that surrounded the chortens. Known as the "Mani Game," it was a crazy and perilous sport and the children held flashlights in their hands as they jumped from wall to wall to evade capture. Every now and then we saw a body tumbling from one of the walls and held our breaths expecting the worst to happen. It was amazing how no one got so much as a bruise.

It was such a pleasant friendly valley that it seemed a shame not to stay and rest for a while. No one was in any hurry to pack and after a very leisurely breakfast Sarah and Bridget Kellas went off sketching. Peter sat down at the side of the chorten and wrote up his diary and the rest of us just lay around sunning ourselves. Only the doctors had work to do—when a dozen of the local people gathered for medical attention.

Rather reluctantly we climbed up a pleasantly graded hillside to the crest of a pass at nine thousand feet. Ahead of us we could see the track winding over rolling hills and there was only an occasional glimpse of a snowy peak. We felt a little sad that the high mountains were now far behind us.

In a few hours we were walking through the busy and crowded town of Those. The narrow streets were paved with cobblestones and lined with smelly open drains, while above us the jumbled houses leaned drunkenly across the street, completely hiding the sun from the murky alleys. Dogs and chickens ran helter-skelter all around us, and on both sides were lines of shops carrying strange mixtures of merchandise. The friendly welcoming smiles of the mountain people had gone and we were back to the interested but impersonal stare of townsfolk.

One shop intrigued me greatly. Called "The Paper Shop" in English lettering, it displayed great piles of local paper which was made from the strong and stringy bark of the daphne bush. It looked a little like pale brown rice paper and I would dearly have loved to buy a large bundle, but Ed hated the yapping dogs and the filth and told us to hurry along. On the edge of town we passed the Those school and in very parochial fashion criticized its uneven roof—not nearly as well built as our Sherpa schools we thought—but it was certainly a large building and would hold a lot of children.

Toward the end of the day's march we had to cross a long suspension bridge, a particularly wobbly one with just one narrow plank for a walkway. Mingma dispatched the Sherpas to escort us over the bridge, but by now the children were so sure of foot that they ran unconcernedly across before the Sherpas could help them.

As I walked down the valley in the bright afternoon sun there was plenty of time to think, and to look at the pleasant countryside around us. Surely there cannot be many places in Asia where people lead a better life. Their whitewashed houses looked comfortable and prosperous, set in snug little gardens with patches of vegetables, chili plants, orange and peach and banana trees, and surrounded by the family's rice fields. They suffer from lack of medical help, education, unscrupulous moneylenders, and the like, but on the whole their life seems happy, secure, and not too arduous.

We spent the night beside the river a few miles below the town of Those. It was a windy spot but open and sunny, with plenty of room for tents on a farmer's disused field. In a halfhearted fashion I ordered my family to wash in the river and then realized that we were back in so-called civilization with Those a few miles above us. The water could well be contaminated, so tooth cleaning was forgotten for the time being.

Ang Passang and Ang Tsering started preparing the evening's chicken curry—our usual diet, as a couple of scrawny cocks could easily be purchased at the end of each day's march. As our Sherpas were devout Buddhists there was always the problem of killing the birds.

"Lama Sahib, Lama Sahib," we heard Ang Tsering calling, "will you kill chickens tonight?"

"Lama Sahib" was the Sherpas' affectionate nickname for Mike Gill, who being twenty-eight years old should by Sherpa standards have been married with children. But Mike was at that moment completely absorbed in smoking his first Biri, a local cigarette made of a rough type of tobacco rolled in a leaf and tied very delicately with a piece of cotton. With a twinkle in his eye, Ang Tsering decided to attract his attention by elevating him to the Buddhist peerage.

"Rimpoche (reincarnate one)," he bellowed, "Rimpoche Sahib, it is time to kill chickens!" This had the desired effect and Mike leaped to his feet and got on with the job.

The nine children had turned into a rather crazy gang over the previous few days. As there were no mani walls to play among, they developed a new game called "Lurky" which occupied all their evening. The general idea was to lurk unseen in a shadowy corner, with intermittent wild dashes over walls, rocks, and ditches. All this necessitated risking life and limb, but we parents were quite oblivious to the suicidal tendencies of our children and sat peacefully by the fire. It was a perfectly clear night and we watched a satellite hustle across the sky and listened to Sherpas singing in the distance.

Next morning I woke to the awful realization that this was our last day of trekking in the Himalayas and felt sad and depressed. While we breakfasted, a very irate Nepalese gentleman appeared at the camp and berated our Sherpas for using a pile of his stakes as firewood. He said that he was returning to Those immediately and would send a policeman to deal with us.

"Is it true that you used the stakes for firewood?" Ed asked Mingma.

"Yes, Burrah Sahib, it is true, but it was all a mistake. Some children came to the camp and we gave them empty cans. In return they offered to bring us some firewood, which, after we had burned it, turned out to be the farmer's stakes." We waited for some time, almost hoping that a policeman would come, but after two rather official-looking gentlemen had walked past our camp without stopping, we decided it was time to start traveling once more. We were loading up all our porters when another man drew near our camp, hesitated, and then carried on. He may well have been the local policeman, who, on see-ing our large and boisterous party, decided that in such a minor matter discretion was possibly the better part of valor.

Ahead of us was only five miles of easy walking to the Swiss Aid Center of Jiri. On the way we passed a delight-ful little settlement of four houses set among beautiful pine trees.

"Who lives there?" I asked Mingma.

"Chetri people, very rich, not strong, so no good," he said. "They eat no meat or eggs and make much money." Nepal with all its beauty is still a divided country, for as well as the division of the Sherpa Buddhist people and the Hindu Nepalese people there are many other subdivi-sions of tribes and customs.

CHAPTER 15

Down to Earth

....

The Swiss Technical Aid farm at Jiri was a little bit of Switzerland transplanted to Nepal. Similar houses and buildings can be seen in any Swiss valley, complete with cobblestone paths and courtyards. The fertile fields and wide variety of crops showed the beneficial result of experienced farming practices, and there was an air of productivity and contentment over the whole valley.

We were welcomed to this Shangri-La by a pleasant group of Nepalese workers, who escorted us to a camping ground carpeted with thick soft grass, not far from the airfield. It was sad to think that our trek was now truly finished and we would have to say good-bye to many of our Sherpa friends. Ed worked out some complicated sums, adding up weights of freight and passengers for Katmandu, and came to the conclusion that the Twin Pioneer would have to make two flights to move us the next day—much to our delight, as this meant some spare space for Sherpas who wanted a holiday visit to Katmandu.

Sherpas from all directions came running to stake their claims for a free ride, and Ed with the help of Mingma sorted out the lucky passengers. Ang Dawa came gamboling up. "Please, Sahib, please, Sahib," he said, his face wreathed in smiles.

"No, Ang Dawa," Mingma said very firmly, "you always get into trouble in Katmandu and lose all your money. You must go back to Phortse." Poor Ang Dawa's face fell, but Ed had to agree. In Katmandu he would have spent all his money on useless things and on an orgy of eating.

"You must spend some of your money on clothing for yourself and your wife . . . and get some furniture for your house," said Ed. Ang Dawa grinned shyly and nodded his head in agreement. Mingma spoke very firmly in Sherpa and there was a roar of laughter from the crowd. "What did you say, Mingma?"

"I told him not to spend so much money on big eating. Two plates of rice enough. Three plates of rice too much!"

In the end everything worked itself out quite well. Of our special friends among the Sherpas only Ang Tsering and Ang Dawa were returning home immediately, so our farewells were going to be gradual and not too painful. We now felt free to sort our gear for the last time, and in traditional expedition fashion we gave away everything we could spare to our faithful helpers. Everything went— trousers, pajamas, socks, the children's spare toys and castoff clothing. If the plane had failed to pick us up next day we would have frozen to death.

Most of the Swiss staff were away on furlough or working in different valleys, but in the early evening we were invited to visit the house of the Swiss forestry expert. We sipped a delicious German white wine and discussed our mutual interests and problems. It was great fun and we walked back to our tents in a pleasant glow of good fellowship.

That night the Sherpas put on a grand party for us. They built a huge fire and many of their friends and relations, who were working for the Swiss, joined in the fun. They started dancing and singing rather tentatively at first, but Ang Dawa, who had suddenly come to life in the most startling manner, walked around the group of seated Sherpas and roughly pulled them one by one into the dancing. The brilliant frosty air made the sound of their singing reverberate up and down the valley and the stars twinkled down upon us so very brightly that we felt they were coming a little closer to enjoy the entertainment. By midnight we, the onlookers, were so hot on one side from the fire and so completely frozen on the other side from the frosty air that we decided it was high time to go to bed. But the dancing and singing continued well into the early hours of the morning.

Despite our late night, we were out of bed very promptly, to breakfast on large floury boiled potatoes from Junbesi and sweet potatoes as well. The wireless operator from Jiri sent word that Ken Hart would arrive in the Twin Pioneer at 9 A.M. We decided that this was more likely to be 10 A.M., leaving us with a couple of hours to walk up the hill behind Jiri to visit a weekly market called "The Hart." Ed and Max were fully occupied in bundling up equipment for our departure so stayed behind.

"It doesn't look far," said Ed. "Probably take you about ten minutes to walk up the hill in your fit condition. When you see the plane overhead, hurry down to the airstrip. If you run really fast you will be back in five minutes."

We walked up the hill as quickly as we could, but it was still nearly forty minutes before we reached the market. Dozens of people were already spreading out their wares. What an unlikely place it was for a market—a bare flat top of a hill without a house in sight in any direction. Where else in the world would you find people willing to carry their goods to a market on top of a mountain instead of down in a valley, and where else in the world would people go to so much trouble to have their market in the middle of nowhere? Here we were on a great wide ridge with the blue sky all around us and a great chattering crowd of humanity bustling like ants around their nest.

It was the orange season and at least half the merchandise was great bamboo baskets of tangerines and a few smaller mounds of bright yellow lemons. There were the usual basic food requirements such as rice, flour, and interesting piles of rock salt glistening in the sun. We decided to buy oranges, for Mingma said they would be much cheaper here than back in Katmandu. No one had remembered to bring baskets, so we tied knots in the arms of our spare clothing and they served as very satisfactory containers. Everyone bargained madly, trying to outdo one another, and I am sure that the prices at the Jiri market had never rocketed so furiously as they did on this particular day. Suddenly, as Lois was filling up a last Pearl cardigan sleeve with oranges, I saw the plane appear from behind a neighboring ridge.

"The plane, the plane," I screamed. "Run for your lives." Everyone took up the cry and we left the poor sales people staring in astonishment as we whooped our way wildly down the hill. We bumped and slid and left a trail of oranges bouncing along behind us. By now a steady stream of people were coming up to the market and we seemed to be crashing into them all the time.

"Chito, chito (quickly, quickly)," they called to us cheekily as we rushed past them.

"Good-bye," we yelled to anybody who looked at all familiar. Now the plane was making its final approach to the airstrip and we were still hundreds of feet above the valley. Ann slipped and fell on a stone, splitting her trousers almost from top to bottom, and Siku came grunting down with a huge basket of oranges on his shoulder. Ang Dooli, carrying my purse with all my money and passport, was quite a long way behind. I glanced back to see Arthur Kellas drifting down the hillside in amazingly dignified and Ambassadorial fashion, but Bridget came flashing by as if she were competing in an Olympic event. By the time we reached the plane everything was packed and in readiness for departure. We were purple-faced and speechless.

"Get in quickly," we were told. There was no time for more good-byes and we tumbled inside, where there were so many children that some of them had to sit on people's laps. The scene in the plane was one of excited and sweating confusion. The most amusing touch of all came when a very well-dressed Nepalese official climbed on board and sat on the last remaining seat. We all looked so wild and he looked so particularly formal that there was a sudden hush as we tried to smooth down our hair and tidy our clothes a little. The Nepalese Government had introduced a new rule that an official had to travel on each charter flight to ensure that we didn't go anywhere or carry anything that wasn't approved of. I thought he looked rather embarrassed and uncomfortable about it all.

"Everybody O.K.?" Ken Hart yelled.

"I suppose so," someone replied, rather doubtfully, and with that the engines roared and we lurched forward. We leaped down the runway and clawed our way out of the steep-sided valley, slipped round a corner and finally burst into the clear air. In barely half an hour we were descending to Katmandu airport. The transition from the mountains to the city was so sudden that many of us had tears in our eyes. Ann explained our feelings on the subject very clearly when she said, "Every time I think about it, I want to cry."

Our parting from the mountain world was not to be as abrupt as we had feared. Waiting for us on the tarmac was a colorful group of Sherpas. Soon we were hugging old Nima Tashi and his wife from Khumjung and their son Phu Dorje, who was now a Nepalese national hero after reaching the summit of Everest with the Indian Expedition of 1965. They had brought all their friends and relations. Scarves were put around our necks and cup after cup of tea pressed on us from large gaily decorated Chinese thermos flasks.

What a strange scene it was. On our right was a RNAC Fokker Friendship airliner, smart and modern, and beside it was the battered squat Twin Pioneer, steadily dripping oil. Our fit but grubby group, halfway between tears and laughter, was surrounded by cheerful Sherpas mostly dressed in traditional attire. Behind us, looking forgotten and forlorn, was an immaculate black shiny Austin Princess with the Ambassadorial Union Jack flapping sadly in the wind.

Most of the Hillarys and Kellases managed somehow to squeeze themselves into the spacious elegance of the Austin. Somebody held Blackie on his knee and we waved good-bye to our friends as our smartly dressed and somewhat disapproving Katmandu chauffeur drove us slowly onto the main road to the city. I don't know if it was our luxurious surroundings or a bad conscience, but we all felt particularly itchy. It was probably Blackie's fault. As we drove back we discussed various means whereby we could change our clothes before entering the Embassy grounds and leave our fleas and any other insect life outside. We soon forgot about it in the excitement of arriving at the Kellas official residence, which was still cheerfully decorated for Christmas. Mr. Kellas had very kindly agreed to let us establish a tent camp for the Sherpas in a pleasant tree-lined corner at the bottom of the garden, and we were delighted to think we could keep our Sherpas with us.

Soon coffee and tea were being served out on the lawn and Siku and Tenzing Niendra were being introduced to tea drinking, British Embassy style. A couple of Embassy servants dressed in neat white uniforms handed them dainty porcelain cups filled with tea from a silver tea service. The cups looked decidedly fragile in such tough and battered hands, but our Sherpas maintained the quiet but impressive dignity which is so much a part of their makeup. The servants were a little ill at ease with our rough and smelly party but carried on nobly in well-trained style. The only person put out by the day's adventures was Blackie, who was promptly sick in the middle of the lawn.

"He's probably carsick," Sarah remarked. We all decided this must be so and let it go at that.

The dreaded moment of unpacking and cleaning up couldn't be put off any longer. It was sad to think that once the nice smoky layer of dirt was removed, the spell— and the smell—of the Himalayas would be gone forever. There were four bathrooms in the Embassy and they were used until the last drop of hot water had disappeared. By that time everyone was clean and a few shades paler. When we gathered for lunch in the dining room we eyed each other in our strange new city clothes with a certain amount of distrust. Everyone looked overdressed and uncomfortable in clothes that hung baggily from loss of weight. The large roast dinner that we soon demolished must have quickly started to fill out our bony frames.

We spent a week in Katmandu. Most of it seemed to be spent in cleaning up equipment and clothes and packing expedition gear, for there was much that had to be sent back to New Zealand and other things that were being left behind for later programs. Quite a lot of the washing

I did myself, for the "dhobi" washed so enthusiastically that I thought some of our well-worn garments might never return in one piece. I'd take my wet washing down to the bottom of the garden to the Sherpas' camp and they'd help dry it on the branches of trees and hedges.

We all worked very hard over these few days, but in the evenings many of our friends entertained us. On the second evening of our stay we went to a picture party for the Embassy staff and children. Our host, a bachelor, lived in part of an old palace. His apartment was cold and echoing but filled with many beautiful Nepalese and Tibetan artifacts. One distinctive feature of the establishment was the extraordinary ratio of one bedroom to two colossal and cavernous bathrooms. Unfortunately Belinda had run a slight temperature during the day so I put her into a sleeping bag and brought her along. She sat in state on a large armchair while the rest of the children ran around exploring the amazing bathrooms. When it was time for the films we were escorted into the bedroom, which had been turned into a small theater. First we watched the everyday doings of a pop group in northern England who spent their days and nights strumming hysterically on their instruments while teenagers screamed and swooned. This was so incongruous in our present environment that even the children of the audience hissed and whistled in high glee.

The St. Trinian Train Robbery was the main film of the evening and we laughed and cheered our way through an impossible story set in green and pleasantly traditional England. It was late by the time the film finished and we hungrily filed into the dining room for a superb meal. My mind was not on the delicious curry and salad, though, for I was worried about Belinda, whose temperature had risen quite considerably in the last hour. She had become restless and spent her time rushing along the cold stone passage in her thin pajamas and bare feet. I am ashamed to say that it was not until eleven-thirty that we put our ailing daughter to bed.

The adventures of the night that followed have been experienced by many parents when they are far away from home. Ed relegated himself to the children's room so that Belinda could be near me, and I didn't have long to wait before trouble started. At about one-thirty in the morning I was wakened by a coughing sound. When I switched on the light I was confronted with the depressing picture of Belinda being violently sick in her sleep. It was a freezing cold night so I hastily donned my Himalayan down jacket and cleaned up as best I could. Then off to sleep once more.

About an hour and a half later I woke to hear Belinda sobbing quietly to herself. This time she had soiled the bed at the other end and after surveying the damage it was quite obvious that no part of Belinda's bed was habitable, so I dressed her in a pair of Peter's pajamas, which was all that was left, and put her in my bed, surrounded by the last towels from the bathroom. As I lay waiting for the next emergency I decided that her rise in temperature earlier in the day must have been the beginnings of a sharp bout of dysentery. When the blessed early light of dawn found its way into our room, Belinda and I were wedged uncomfortably across one corner of the bed, which was all that was left clean and pure.

At the breakfast table I looked distinctly bleary-eyed.

"What's wrong with you?" Ed said. "It can't have been as bad as all that. You must have got a few hours of rest."

"Well I did," I replied, "but most of them were spent at the bottom of the bed not daring to move for fear of disturbing Belinda."

Back upstairs I had the embarrassing experience of watching the Embassy staff tidying up our bedroom. The two servants slowly stripped Belinda's bed and as they delved deeper and deeper still, finding everything soiled, they looked at me accusingly, as if to say, "How could you!" Finally, to my great relief, they departed with the great pile of bed linen and blankets. With the help of some tablets prescribed by Max, Belinda recovered in three days, but when she left her sick bed, her bony legs and arms worried me considerably.

On the night after the picture party, the Embassy held a cocktail party for an important English visitor. The usual invitations to Nepalese officials and diplomats were sent out, but the Kellases had completely fallen in love with the Sherpa people and decided to ask all their Sherpa friends as well. They accepted the invitation with alacrity and rushed to the house of Everest climber Phu Dorje, who was experienced in such matters, and asked his advice about what to wear. When they arrived in company with the foreign diplomats and important Nepalese citizens they looked scrubbed and extremely smart. But mountain people can never really submerge their personalities, and Mingma, the intense hard-working leader of men, had put on a clean shirt and well-tailored sports jacket on top of his dirty shirt. His well-groomed appearance was quite ruined by the points of the dirty collar that stuck above his neat clothing with telltale effect. The Sherpa women must have spent many hours combing, oiling, and replaiting their hair but had then placed old brown knitted balaclavas on top of their coiffures in honor of the occasion. Tenzing Niendra, the Kellases' special friend, upheld Sherpa honor and coped with his formal European collar and tie as if he had been wearing them all his life.

Despite these few idiosyncrasies in dress our Sherpas

were an impressive group and I felt a rush of affection each time I saw their beaming faces. There were many people present with better clothes, more money, and higher social position but none who could surpass the Sherpas in dignity, courage, and tough good humor.

Intermingled with this colorful gathering were the nine children of the Hillarys, Pearls, and Kellases, who had been told that they could help. Every now and then I had to close my eyes in horror as one of my children would struggle through the crowd holding a heavily laden tray of expensive cut crystal glasses, but there were no casualties. The Sherpa women were very impressed with both the handsome reception rooms and the children in their party clothes.

We had no sooner let Belinda out of bed than Peter developed bronchitis. He wasn't very sick but was tired and miserable and most thankful to stay in bed. Meanwhile Belinda dashed around the Embassy compound looking like a starving child, but judging by the way she was tucking into her food again it would only be a matter of days and she would be back to normal.

More of our hospitable Katmandu friends had invited us to spend the evening with them, but I didn't know what to do with Peter while he was unwell. Mingma decided that Siku and Pemba Tarkay could come and sit with him while we were away. Peter was having difficulty with his breathing when we departed, so I explained to the Sherpas that he probably wouldn't want to talk or play. They sat down on a couple of chairs facing his bed, with very serious expressions on their faces. When we returned three hours later the Sherpas were still sitting in exactly the same position, and I have never seen such a look of relief on Peter's face before or since.

"How did you get on?" we asked.

"All right," was the noncommittal reply.

"Thank you, Pemba Tarkay. Thank you, Siku," I said.

"That's all right, Memsahib," they both chorused and hurried out of the room.

"What happened?" I asked Peter.

"Well, it was actually terribly funny. Neither of the Sherpas dared speak to me, and they sat there for the first half hour without moving. Then Mingma came in, and all three sat and looked at me except for the odd occasion when I moved and then Siku leaped up and brought me a plastic basin, for he seemed to think that I was about to vomit. Mingma looked rather bored, so he tried the new prayer wheel to pass the time."

"Oh, did he?" I said. "Well, that was very nice. What did he do exactly."

"He picked it up, bowed his head, and touched his forehead with it, and then stared at me while he twirled the wheel and mumbled prayers. I wondered if perhaps he thought I was going to die. After he had done that for about a quarter of an hour he put the prayer wheel back in its place and left the room. Soon after this Pemba Tarkay fell asleep in his chair but quickly woke up with a jolt. He stopped himself from falling asleep again by looking through all our drawers. Siku was feeling bored too, and he saw a bottle of pills on the table, took a couple out and munched them with a look of satisfaction on his face."

"What on earth were they?" I asked.

"I don't know. They don't seem to have a label."

"Well, we must ask Max tomorrow. Let's hope he lives through the night. What happened after that?" I asked.

"Well, they just sat and stared at me with worried faces until you came in. That's why I was so pleased when you returned."

There was one more very important social occasion during our stay in Katmandu and that was the combined birthday party of Roger Kellas and Belinda. Their birthdays were only a couple of days apart. Guests were hardly necessary, for there were nine children already, plus their parents and immediate friends who lived in the Embassy compound. A magnificent birthday cake was made for each child and both Roger and Belinda were the lucky recipients of fascinating Nepalese gifts. To entertain the guests, Roger and Ian put on a series of masterly conjuring tricks, all of which succeeded brilliantly until the last one, which needed audience participation. As Belinda was the birthday girl, they asked her to help them, but when she was asked to add up some sums she got all the answers wrong and turned the final trick into glorious disorder.

The New Zealand children then stood up and performed their Maori dancing repertoire and the program finished with Miranda reciting a collection of nonsense poems.

The next day was a sad day. Our trekking party was becoming smaller and smaller, for the three Kellas children had to leave us and fly back to school in England. After the children had left for Delhi with their mother, everything seemed a little quiet and the boisterous Blackie had disappeared.

"Where's Blackie?" one of the children asked.

"He's with the Sherpas, I think," Ed replied. So they rushed off to get him. A few minutes later they returned.

"Look, isn't he sweet?" Belinda said. "He won't wake up." We all crowded round to look. Our funny little black bouncing ball of fluff lay like a forgotten rag toy with his tiny red tongue sticking out of his mouth.

"How sweet," everyone said. "But shouldn't we wake him?"

"Yes, wake him up," everyone chorused, suddenly becoming rather worried. So Belinda shook him.

"Shake him harder." But nothing happened.

"Was he like this when you found him?" Ed inquired.

"Yes, he was lying in one of the tents," said Peter. "It was very hot and he didn't move. We thought he'd been drugged by the heat." Suddenly the little dog let out a moan and his whole body was torn by a horrible convulsion. This was terribly alarming; we didn't want anything going wrong with Blackie. He had been through so many adventures with us and was about to be adopted by the Kellas family as a household pet.

"Get one of the doctors! Quickly!" I said. We sent for Mike, who lived in the house next door, but he wasn't at home, so Max was sent for. Blackie was examined with great care and everybody stood round with strained and worried faces.

"He's had a fit," said Max in sepulchral tones, "and is now in a coma."

"Will he be all right?" was the instant cry.

"I don't know," said Max. "He might never wake up." Then someone remembered that Flicka Kinear, wife of the first secretary of the British Embassy and kindly hostess of the Pearl family, was a vet. The limp black puppy was scooped up and rushed to the Kinear household. Flicka didn't seem too hopeful when she saw the small patient.

"Keep him warm," she advised, so a couple of shirts were hastily offered as temporary blankets.

"He's had a fit because he has bad worms." We all gasped with relief. "But," she went on, "he still mightn't come out of the coma."

"What can we do?" we asked.

"Well, he might be brought round with a little brandy and then he must have some good protein food." This was soon done, and then we tried to feed him a little sponge cake. But he immediately sagged back into his coma

and looked very much as though he was dying. I heard a
deep sighing sob come from one of the spectators and
turned round to see that Sarah had burst into bitter tears.
All our Sherpas were very upset, for they were equally attached to Blackie and they stood in dejected groups waiting for news of his condition. We packed Blackie into a
cardboard carton surrounded by as much warm clothing
as we could gather, and Ang Dooli offered to mind him.

We left him in her capable hands and took the children
shopping in the bazaar in an attempt to cheer them up.
The next day was our last in Katmandu and I had promised Dianne McKinnon that I would send her up some necessities for the hospital housekeeping and her school
work. We combed the busy bazaars for large sheets of thick
drawing paper, colored pencils, scrubbing brushes, tins for
baking loaves of bread, and various other odds and ends.
Then we bought the provisions we would need when we
continued our travels. The afternoon had been well spent,
but as soon as we returned to the Embassy our thoughts
immediately turned to Blackie. He was still alive but in a
deep coma.

"Oh dear," said one of the children, "how are we going
to live through the next few hours until we know what's
going to happen to him?"

As soon as we woke next day we immediately remembered Blackie. Would he be alive or dead? Our children,
with suitably funereal looks on their faces, wandered down
the garden to find out the dreadful truth. What a wonderful sight met their eyes! The tough, rough Blackie had survived, in fact he had survived so well that on seeing the
children he rushed at them and attacked them in his usual
fierce way. To celebrate the event Blackie was handed over
to his new keepers, the staff at the Embassy residence. Ram
Bahadur, the head bearer, couldn't conceal his pleasure

at having a dog in the household and we knew that Blackie would be very happy in his new home. In fact he celebrated his recovery by making a mess on the dining-room carpet and we hoped sincerely that we would manage to get away from Katmandu before the Kellas household changed their minds and decided against having Blackie after all.

No visit to Katmandu would be complete without a little time spent searching in its old bazaars and those of the adjoining and ancient city of Patan. Lois and I spent a very happy morning being guided by two experienced and knowledgeable friends. We spent hours in the little back streets, where we found tiny curio shops, only frequented by the most enthusiastic treasure hunters. I was full of admiration for Maria, our friend and driver for the morning. She drove her Landrover round the tiny narrow streets of Katmandu valley like a professional—no street was too narrow for her and no tumultuous crowd of heedless people could intimidate her. She apparently thought that Lois and I must be of the same tough breed, for when we were irrevocably stopped by a large cow sitting in the middle of the street she asked us very nicely to get out and move it. Much to our relief, a kindly Nepali gentleman gave the cow a hearty kick and we were able to continue on our way.

Our visit to the bazaars had left me in a buying frame of mind, so that afternoon Ed and I, with the help of Boris and Inger Lissanovitch (of Royal Hotel fame), bought a picture. Katmandu attracts artists and there are a bewildering number of canvases to feast your eyes on. The painting that attracted us was of Katmandu valley backed by Himalayan peaks. It was a bright sunlit picture of pagoda-like temples and little houses shining in the clear Himalayan air. The artist had used an energetic palette knife and the result was gay and strong, just as we would like to remember Katmandu. It was only after we had paid the money to Mr. Gujer, the Indian artist, that we realized that our new picture measured two feet by four feet and was not on a canvas but on a large piece of hardboard. How were we going to get it back to New Zealand?

"I don't mind carrying it into the airplane and hiding it somewhere," I said hopefully. Ed agreed that this would be quite possible as long as I promised to pretend that I wasn't related to him.

"But what about our drive down to India tomorrow, and then our train ride across northern India to Darjeeling?" I said.

"We'll manage somehow," was the laconic reply, and we did.

CHAPTER 16

The King's Road

··

When Nepal was first opened to the outside world in 1950 the only way to get to Katmandu was on foot or on horseback. Ed's descriptions of journeys by train across India followed by the two-day walk over the steeply terraced hills of Nepal always sounded very romantic.

"The trains are really quite comfortable, you know, and it's a fascinating way to see the scenery. Whenever the train stops at a station, vendors walk back and forth crying out their wares: 'Garam pani!' (hot water) 'Garam dudh!' (hot milk) 'Garam char!' (hot tea). It's all very noisy but terribly colorful. I know you'd love it!" Ed insisted.

My only glimpses of the Nepalese foothills up until now were from a plane flying at an altitude of about twelve thousand feet, and I had never traveled on an Indian train.

Katmandu became far less isolated when the Indian Government built a brilliantly engineered road through to the city from the plains of India. It was called the "Raj Path" (King's Road) and we'd heard so much about its spectacular scenery that the Hillary and Pearl families decided on this occasion they must travel out to India by car and then across India by train.

Ed contacted a Nepalese agency, appropriately called

"Everest Travel," and asked them to make bookings for sixteen of us. There were the ten members of the two families; Mike Gill; Mingma and Ang Dooli; Siku and Pemba Tarkay, who were being given a holiday trip to Darjeeling; and Tenzing Niendra, who wanted to visit some relations in Assam. We were particularly happy to be accompanied by so many Sherpas, as it meant fewer farewells in Katmandu.

Our travel agent had been rather alarmed at the number in our party but nevertheless presented us with all our tickets a couple of days before our departure. When we studied them carefully it appeared that during our twenty-four-hour train trip from Raxaul across northern India to Siliguri, the railhead for Darjeeling, we would be changing trains three times during the night.

"Can't something else be done?" we inquired.

"No, nothing. It is quite impossible," said the travel agent. "You are having to travel on small branch lines and there is nothing I can do."

"Let's cancel it all," said Ed. I was amazed, for he is by far the most adventurous member of our family.

"Never!" I said. "If we don't do this trip now we'll never have time to do it on any other occasion." We had a meeting of all the people involved and decided that, as we had four able and trusty Sherpa friends to help us, it was definitely worth a try.

Early on a frosty, misty morning in the middle of January, our party of sixteen packed ourselves into one car and three jeeps in readiness for our new adventure. We were accompanied by twenty-eight pieces of baggage, one large painting, and a bulky and very breakable earthenware water jar that I was determined to take back to New Zealand. We were so crammed with luggage and people that Pemba Tarkay and Siku had to sit half in and half out of the last overladen vehicle.

We said our sad good-byes to the Sherpas we were leaving behind and to our many kind friends in the Embassy and then before we could burst with our emotion Ed poked his head out of the car and told the convoy to be on its way. With a tooting of horns, much grinding of gears, and some frantic waving we left the Embassy compound behind us. The last figure I saw as we passed through the gates was the dignified head servant, Ram Bahadur, standing in the front door of the Embassy with a black fluffy thing under his arm, wriggling and waggling its tail in farewell.

"Good-bye, Blackie, good-bye, Blackie," chorused all the children from different vehicles.

Our noisy convoy rattled through the sleeping, mist-dulled streets of Katmandu, over the Bhagmati river, and finally out into the countryside. We drove across the Katmandu valley between tiny checkerboard winter fields and neat little plastered houses with attractive tiled roofs. It was the personification of a neat, uncomplicated, orderly life. In this world of change, warfare, and misunderstanding it was reassuring to see such things. Long may Nepal live in peace!

Just before leaving the valley there was a checkpost for foreigners. We unfolded ourselves carefully from the cars rather like football players after a tackle and pile-up. The checkpost officers welcomed us like party guests, for I think we were their first customers for the morning. Mike, who loves to try any food or drink, took this opportunity to have an early morning cup of tea from a little roadside stall. With the formalities quickly over, we chugged our way up to a pass at six thousand feet. We stopped to have a last look back at the valley with its protective wall of great

white peaks sparkling in the early rays of the sun, and then
into the cars once more.

Ahead of us was row after row of winter-brown mountains dissected by the incredible corkscrew thread of the
Raj Path leading south toward India. We felt pleasantly
excited, but nervous, like swimmers about to take their
first plunge into icy water.

Down the hill we went for several thousand feet, zigzagging our way around tight sharp corners. The sealed
surface was in very good order and we were filled with admiration for the Indian engineers who had built this road
in such steep country. Then up the other side again along
incredibly abrupt mountain slopes. The ever-changing
scenes were stupendous in size and glorious in color. The
soft pastel browns and golds stretched as far as the eye
could see. Neat little houses and terraced fields perched
all over the landscape.

To the north the white toothlike peaks of the Himalayas
managed to peep over the ever-increasing lines of foothills. Waving fronds of delicate bamboo, and other trees,
made wonderful foregrounds for our views across the deep
valleys. I was determined to take a picture with bamboo
in the foreground and hazy mountains behind, but every
time I saw a suitable place we would go swooping round a
steep bend with such urgency that I hardly had time to
breathe.

Mr. Gurung, our driver, always took the lead in our
convoy and at times would get too far ahead. We found
his habit of looking behind for the other vehicles a little
nerve-racking and hoped he wouldn't drive off the road.

"I'm a Darjeeling driver, you know," he said, "and very
much more experienced on these mountain roads. The
other drivers are all Katmandu valley drivers and haven't

got any idea of how to cope with an icy surface." We all made a mental note to stay with Mr. Gurung.

We didn't lose any of our convoy, even though Siku lost his breakfast on a very twisty section of the road. When we stopped to let him recover, he looked as green as the clumps of dainty bamboo on the hillsides, and Ang Dooli's face was just about as unhealthy. We rearranged the seating and put the two green-looking passengers in more comfortable front seats.

The road had been so deeply cut into the precipitous slopes that great slips had occurred, obliterating acres and acres of narrow terraced fields. We wondered vaguely what sort of compensation the local people would get for this. One such slip appeared to stretch unendingly below us and we crossed it gingerly on a ledge of unstable mud.

There was quite a lot of traffic on the Raj Path, mostly buses and trucks. Every now and then we would see someone held up with engine trouble. One of these unfortunates was a great friend of Mr. Gurung's and we stopped for a long cheering conversation.

"Poor man," our driver said, "he has been there for four days waiting for spare parts."

"What can he do?" we said in horror.

"Oh, just sit about," said Mr. Gurung. "He would be quite content talking to the people who live nearby." What a different approach to life! We Westerners are such an impatient lot that we could never have put up with waiting around for four days.

To reach India we had to cross a high pass of eight thousand feet. We drove toward it, up a wide and verdant valley—a green oasis with three or four villages and many acres of fertile ground. The inhabitants seemed fairly prosperous and their houses were brightly painted, some in the most astounding and unusual colors. Already in the background we could hear the inevitable mutterings of "When can we have lunch?"

"If you wait a while," said Mr. Gurung to the children, "we come to a lovely place on the ridge at about seven thousand feet where there is a proper picnic spot."

"We don't want a proper picnic spot," was the reply.

"Oh, but this is very beautiful, and it has a shelter and lookout and everybody goes there," said Mr. Gurung enthusiastically. He was right about its being a good spot. We stopped the cars and climbed up above the road for about twenty feet to a memorial plaque for the builders of the Raj Path. As we looked north we could see the Himalayas stretching for at least a hundred miles or more.

"There's Everest," someone yelled.

"There's Gauri Sanka."

"I think we can almost see down to Kanchenjunga," said Ed.

"Let's have lunch here right now," said Sarah, who was always reminding us that food was uppermost in her mind.

"No! We must go to the shelter provided," said Mr. Gurung. He was clearly so proud of the shelter that we agreed to cooperate. We returned to the cars and chugged a few yards farther uphill to some large and solid concrete steps leading to a tall white concrete tower with a round glassed-in lookout room at the top. We had company at the lookout—a party of four Russians, who looked at us distrustfully, even though we tried to be friendly, and three very pale and shy Japanese tourists. You could hardly blame the Russians for their lack of enthusiasm, for we were a noisy and cheerful group and we arrived with four large cartons of food, including two dozen cans of beer. The Russians were not to know that these provisions had to last until we reached Darjeeling in three days' time, and to their eyes we must have looked like overfed imperialists all set for a wild party. To add to this bad impression we had six large gin bottles of distilled water for mixing with orange squash.

When we asked our drivers if they would like to lunch with us, Mr. Gurung answered for them all by saying that they never bothered about food when driving and would stop later in the day for a meal of curry. Feeling decidedly greedy, we attacked our food with enthusiasm—fresh bread and butter, jam, cheese, and canned salmon, washed down with a can of beer. It was delicious. Everything combined to stimulate our appetites—the fresh cool air, the warm sun, the stunted trees and worn rocks, and the glorious mountain views.

I was expecting the final climb to the eight-thousand-foot pass to be steep and nerve-racking, but the skillful grading of the road made it surprisingly easy. On the pass we entered a different world of cold swirling mists, gnarled lichen-covered fir trees, rhododendrons, and sweet-smelling daphne. We wasted no time in this drafty spot and made our way down a series of awe-inspiring loops until abruptly, we realized that the true Nepalese countryside was now irrevocably behind us. The vegetation took on a tropical and untidy appearance and the houses became makeshift and ramshackle. Down and down we went, leaving the fresh mountain air behind, getting covered with dust and feeling hot and sticky.

We were all in need of a wash and a respite from the cramped and stuffy cars. Our main hope for this was at the U. S. Aid Depot at Hitaura. The American Ambassador, Miss Laise, had offered us the use of it and assured us we would find it most adequate. As we drove through the main gate of the depot we blessed Miss Laise for her thoughtfulness.

"I wonder where the guesthouse is," I murmured softly to myself, envisioning some fantastic and luxurious American apartment with hot and cold water, soft white linen towels, and delicious cool refreshments. There didn't seem to be anybody about on this quiet Sunday afternoon, but a sleepy gentleman finally appeared after much knocking on various doors and we asked him to take us to the guesthouse.

"Follow me," he said with ceremony, and he led us to some tired-looking, railway station type, rest rooms.

"I don't think you heard," I said, slightly hopeful. "Isn't there a guesthouse?"

"This is it," he said with hurt pride.

"Oh, it's very nice," I said. "Thank you so much." But it was too late for me to cover up my disappointment. In rather huffy fashion he showed us a very basic cooking and mess area, told us to make ourselves at home, and, having thus discharged his duties, hastily departed to continue his Sunday afternoon siesta.

As soon as he was out of earshot we gave way to roars of laughter, for this U. S. Aid Depot was a hard-working, down-to-earth place with no time or money wasted on luxuries and I am sure it would never have occurred to Miss Laise that we would have expected otherwise.

There were two large refrigerators in the kitchen and we looked inside them hopefully. To our joy we saw dozens of inviting soft drinks, but firmly written on the door of each refrigerator was a notice saying that the contents belonged to the station staff.

"Oh well, there's nothing for it," I said. "We'll have to walk down to the town and buy some fruit." Just before we left I noticed Tenzing Niendra refilling his water bottle with filtered water from a container in the kitchen.

The little town was a desperately poor and depressing

place and the people were poor and miserable also. Food seemed more or less nonexistent, but we bought a few overripe bananas and three green pawpaws. When we returned to our U. S. Aid kitchen we found that it was fifty per cent under water, as Tenzing Niendra had forgotten to turn off the filter tap.

"Let's eat the pawpaws first and clean up after," one of the men very sensibly suggested.

"Wash your hands before you touch any food," called both mothers and we started to devour the unappetizing and rubbery fruit. The black seeds slid all over the place and by the time we had finished there was a pretty awful mess on the floor. Luckily we found a mop and cleaned everything up as thoroughly as possible.

Our convoy had been driving and looking at views nonstop since 7 A.M. in the morning. It was now 3:30 P.M. and our bright enthusiasm of the morning had disappeared. We continued on over flat country, some of it consisting of unproductive-looking fields and the rest forested and quite beautiful.

"I'll get you to Raxaul at four o'clock, which will give you plenty of time at the immigration and customs posts," said Mr. Gurung.

The Indian border runs right through the center of Raxaul and as we entered the Nepalese side of the town, we found the main road crammed with creaking oxcarts laden with great piles of sugar cane and with the Indian drivers sitting on top.

It was "rush hour." When we reached a bridge in the center of the town the road was impossibly congested with oxcarts, buses, cars, and many trishaws and pedestrians. There appeared to be a hopeless traffic jam and we clambered out of our cars to have a look at the confusion. In the middle of the bridge, and completely blocking it, was a heavily laden oxcart that had lost a wheel. Three small Indians were trying pathetically to move the heavy load and about a hundred onlookers stood passively watching them. Outside this group, infuriated drivers of trishaws, cars, and buses hooted hysterically, knowing full well that their tooting wasn't helping the situation one bit. Suddenly the dreadful realization that we had lost one of our vehicles penetrated our minds. It was the jeep containing Pemba Tarkay and Siku and all our especially valuable luggage.

"We'll never get on the train tonight," I moaned to no one in particular. What a place to have to spend a night! Just across the bridge was the Indian border, so we strolled over with passports to see if we could get a few things organized while the bridge remained blocked. We found a dilapidated shed which housed one overworked Indian Immigration official. There was a great crowd of people pushing and shoving in front of the door so we stood together blocking the entrance in hopes that we might finally force our way in. When we burst into the office, the man in charge looked in horror at our large group.

"Did you see a yellow Russian jeep with two passengers go by a little while ago?" we inquired.

Yes, he had. What a relief! Where they were now, heaven only knew, but at least this might be one less load of gear to be checked by Customs.

"I can't deal with you," said the Immigration Officer, "it would take too long. You must go over to the main office down the street. There Mr. Chattajee, our senior official, will take care of your party. You will get through very much more quickly." We thanked him effusively, and went back to the bridge to see how things were progressing. The situation was still unchanged.

Finally, when the congestion had become quite impossible, the police decided to take a hand. Pushing and shoving, slashing with their sticks in threatening fashion, they cleared some of the onlookers away. By using a long piece of wood as a lever, the Indian drivers lifted the side of the cart and adjusted the wheel. In almost miraculous fashion the cart was dragged off the bridge and traffic started moving again.

We left the children in the cars and told them not to venture out onto the dark and crowded streets, for it would have been so easy to lose one of them. As we walked to the Immigration building a burly policeman barged into me, nearly knocking me over. I felt like pushing him back and only restrained myself with an effort.

"Sit down," said Mr. Chattajee curtly.

"Oh, I don't think we need to sit down," I said hopefully. "We won't be here long." The look I received in reply from Mr. Chattajee was far from encouraging.

"Have you visas?" he said.

"No, we are British citizens."

"Oh," he said, not believing us. He looked carefully through our passports for about ten minutes.

"Who shall I deal with first?" he said, after a long and infuriating pause.

I volunteered. He opened a large and important-looking book and started copying everything in my passport into it. Every now and then his pen would run out of ink. He would slowly and methodically dip it into the ink pot once more. His writing was provokingly slow and he asked me all sorts of questions that were already answered in the passport. After ten minutes of this he had finished with me and it was Lois's turn. To our horror he turned to the next page in his records book which was completely bare, took a ruler and a pencil and very slowly and precisely started ruling lines ready for the next interview. He occupied at least another five minutes with this task while we were all thinking of our tired children sitting by themselves in the cars on the street. After another interminable ten minutes Lois was finished, but there still remained the three men. That meant another half hour with an extra ten minutes thrown in for ruling of pages. But Mr. Chattajee was enjoying himself and when he came to Ed's passport he was fascinated by all the places that Ed had visited. He looked through the passport as if it was a lovely picture book, savoring every new and foreign stamp with utter joy. Slowly he turned page after page, as we watched with almost overwhelming irritation.

"When were you last in England?" he snapped at Ed, and Ed who really is the most patient soul on this earth quietly told him.

"It's all irrelevant. It's all irrelevant," I kept muttering to Ed under my breath.

"Keep quiet," he muttered back, "or we'll be here till midnight."

"Thank you so much, Mr. Chattajee," we all chorused as the last passport was handed back to us.

"You must now go to the Customs Officer across the street," he said.

The Customs Officer turned out to be a hundred times worse than Mr. Chattajee. He was a most difficult man, ugly, unkempt, and rough. When we entered his office he was dealing with a confused and terrified Tibetan woman. She wanted to come into India, but her papers didn't give her date of birth, as she didn't know it. The wretched man was shouting and cursing her so violently that the poor woman had completely lost her head. Luckily our friend and guide Mr. Gurung came to her rescue and managed to sort everything out.

The Customs Officer took my passport and Ed's. He refused to believe that we only had three children between us, for we each had three children mentioned on our separate passports, which added up to six. It wasn't until he started copying down my particulars in his large records book that I realized that he couldn't read English properly. He copied my name down as "Houise Millary" and had a great deal of difficulty in copying down any of the other words. When he had finally satisfied himself that Ed and I did have six children, he opened Ed's passport and started examining it with a look of complete enjoyment on his face. Never had such good entertainment come his way before and he was going to savor it to the utmost.

"We have a train to catch," I told him rather firmly, but he looked at me with complete disinterest. When we finally left his presence we realized that he hadn't even asked us if we had any goods to declare.

There was a strong feeling of bad temper and tiredness in our car. The children had become so restless that in the heat of an argument they had inadvertently emptied the entire contents of my travel bag all over the floor. They had picked everything up as well as they could in the dark, but it was only when I sat down in the car and put my foot under the front seat that I found my precious camera; and it was not until twenty-four hours later that I realized my purse with 125 Indian rupees in it had been left behind.

"Never mind, all will be well," said Ed. "As soon as we get to the station you'll be surprised how things come right. There'll be a comfortable waiting room for us lucky first-class passengers to rest in."

It was a typical Indian railway station with people lying asleep all over the floor, and clusters of thin resigned travelers standing wherever space permitted.

"Where's the toilet, Mum?" somebody asked.

"Oh, I don't know. You'll have to wait."

"But I can't wait," was the answer.

"Well, Daddy will find that nice waiting room soon, don't you worry." But Daddy was far too busy paying off drivers and unloading all our luggage to worry about us. After a few minutes of futile waiting I could see that I would have to take action. Why is it always the mothers that have these problems?

"O.K.," I said to my three children, "I'll find you somewhere, even if it's in the middle of a paddock." We threaded our way onto the station platform and found the ladies room. We wandered inside. The anteroom was covered with sleeping figures. There was a door leading into the toilets, but the stench that came out was rather unwelcoming.

"Well, here you are. This or nothing," I said. So, holding our breaths, we made a dash. There was only one toilet and it was occupied.

"Don't touch anything, you kids," I said. "Keep your hands away from your mouths. Let's retreat." We dashed out and gulped some pure air.

"We'll go outside and find somewhere." So we scuttled round the back of the building past a great pond of smelly water and found ourselves in a wide, open, shadowy, grassy area.

"Right. There you are," I said. "This is your chance."

"We can't go here, Mum, there's too much light," said everybody complainingly.

"All right," I said, "*you* suggest somewhere to go." The odor from the nearby pond was such that no one wanted to venture any farther, so, business concluded, we hurried back inside the station. By this time our party was getting quite well organized. All the luggage had been put in a pile on the platform and our four Sherpa men were guarding it.

"Now for a nice clean Ladies and Gents First Class Waiting Room," said Ed. To my great surprise, he soon came back with the good news that he had found one. We followed him upstairs to a comfortable room inhabited by one prosperous-looking traveler.

"Oh, isn't it lovely," we said. "How long can we stay here? We'll really enjoy this."

Such peace and luxury had never been expected ten minutes before. To celebrate the event, Max produced a large greasy paper bag filled with little cakes that he had bought in Katmandu the day before. I opened one of my cherished bottles of pure filtered water and we had quite a feast. Even Ang Dooli seemed to have recovered a little from the shock of traveling and rather gingerly pecked at a cake.

"Are all the bookings all right?" I inquired. Ed and Max looked slightly uncomfortable.

"The station master says that our first three sections of travel are so short that it is not worth booking seats."

"Oh," I said, "that sounds fun!" And I meant it, for we were embarking on a crazy adventure with enough food to last for at least twenty-four hours, and tents, sleeping bags, air mattresses, and four trusty Sherpas to help us whenever it was necessary.

"What about a meal now?" I inquired.

"Whenever you travel on Indian Railways it's a good idea to have an omelette," said Ed, our guide and technical adviser.

That sounded a sensible idea, so we went to the station dining room. It was not a particularly entrancing or hygienic place, but it was part of Indian Railway travel and therefore had to be experienced. With great bonhomie

Max ordered a dozen omelettes and then handed out a couple of Enterovioform tablets to each member of the party. The waiters, wearing gray bespattered uniforms, vaguely swept a bit of the dirt off the table and soon returned with the omelettes. They sat in great splendor on large stainless steel plates that had been held under a tap briefly after previous use and some of the last meal still clung to them.

"Eat the top of the omelette," I said to my kids, "and keep your hands away from your mouth," I added for about the fiftieth time that day.

The train was due to arrive, so we joined the Sherpas beside the great pile of luggage on the platform. Much to my surprise my beautiful earthenware water jug which had cost me one rupee was still in one piece. It was serving as an excellent container for my collection of Himalayan orchid bulbs. The parcel containing our big picture also seemed to be in good condition, and I devoutly hoped that both these works of art would get through the next twenty-four hours without being seriously damaged.

"Now listen carefully," said Ed. "When the train comes in we will all look for a first-class compartment. When you see one, all the women and children will jump into it as quickly as they can and receive all the luggage that the rest of us pass to them."

We were definitely organizing ourselves for battle, and it only took one glance to understand how real that battle could be. When the train appeared down the line, the huddled, sleeping throng that filled the station came to life and jostled their way unsmilingly and resolutely toward the edge of the platform. It was going to be every man for himself.

By the time the train actually rolled to a standstill our excitement was at fever pitch. Pemba Tarkay, who resembles a lineman in a football game, fought his way bravely into a small first-class compartment and Max and Mike found another one next door. We rushed in and pulled the baggage in after us.

"Twenty-four pieces, twenty-five pieces, twenty-six, twenty-seven. Is that all?"

"What about my water jar?" I screamed.

"Here, Memsahib," said a little voice from the corner. There was Ang Dooli, almost completely wedged in by luggage but triumphantly holding in her hands my still intact treasure.

"Well, everybody must be in the train somewhere," we all agreed. The next thing to do was to make sure that no more people got into our already overcrowded compartment, so we closed the door and put all the luggage in front of it.

"You'd better close the windows too," our experienced train traveler advised. "You'll find the passengers will try anything."

Even when we had sorted out the luggage reasonably well there was very little room for us to sit down. This was quite unimportant, as in less than an hour we would be changing trains at the town of Segouli.

"How will we know when we get to Segouli?" Lois asked.

"Oh, we'll just have to look at all the signs. There'll be no guards to tell us," said Ed. "On these narrow-gauge railways they don't have passageways between carriages for a guard to walk up and down."

"Thank goodness, at least the railway signs are in English," I remarked.

The hour on the train flashed by incredibly swiftly and before we knew it we were in Segouli, with only twenty minutes for our change to the next train. During this short journey we had noticed that Indian Railways tend to stop for as little time as possible at intermediate stations, so it was essential that we develop a brisk workmanlike technique for moving baggage.

My first glance at the Segouli platform was enough to make the stoutest heart quail. The place was a seething, jostling mass of humanity. But the eight burly men of our party seemed to have no trouble in shouldering their way through the crowd, and I'm afraid that Pemba Tarkay in his usual vigorous fashion gave a few swift shoves here and there to hurry our passage.

We had hardly assembled our great mountain of luggage before the next train arrived and immediately a frenzied surge of people pressed forward.

"Keep the children all together and make sure you get on," we were told. A first-class compartment flashed by. Pemba Tarkay leaped after it and boarded it. Half a minute later a poor miserable third-class passenger was pushed firmly out of its doorway.

"Just as a point of interest," I screamed over the din to Ed, "what sort of ticket has Pemba Tarkay got?"

"Third class," he yelled back, with a grin.

We were all aboard once more.

One of my greatest nightmares during this entire train trip was the thought of losing one of the children in this remote part of India. At every stop I'd wildly count my brood. There were people bulging out of the windows and doors of the second- and third-class compartments, and their discomfort appalled me. India is a sad and hard country and we felt almost ashamed to be secluded in our crowded but comfortable first-class compartment. The third-class passengers looked quite resigned to their fate, and as half of them at least had not paid their fares they were only too happy to be sitting anonymously among the jumbled mob of uncomfortable people.

We had three and a half hours before our next battle with the crowds at Muzzaphapur, so sleeping bags were unpacked and all the children were given a seat to lie on. The rest of us propped ourselves up as best we could on pieces of luggage and the ends of seats.

"I think at least two of us should stay awake so we don't miss the station," said Ed.

"Yes, that's a very good idea," I replied. "But who?"

It was decided that Max and Ed would be the unfortunate pair. By this time I was too tired and too cold for sleep anyway and my mind was filled with the nagging worry about missing the next connection. The train rattled its way on through the night.

"I say, Ed," I said all of a sudden, "where are the Garam Pani people and the Garam Dudh people you said would be selling their wares in the warm balmy air of the station platforms?"

"Oh, I don't know," he said rather grumpily. "It may be too late at night." I felt a little cheated as the romanticism and mysticism of the East seemed to be drifting further and further from my grasp.

"Perhaps we'll catch up with it all at the next station," I said.

CHAPTER 17

First-Class Gents

....

After a few hysterical false alarms we finally found Muzzaphapur, at one-twenty in the morning. Even at this hour it appeared a large and busy city and we hastily unloaded ourselves onto the platform. Our train for Baruni Junction didn't leave until 4:45 A.M., so we had the chance of a rest if only we could find a peaceful waiting room. Siku and Pemba Tarkay were told very firmly by Mingma to sit on top of the luggage and guard it for the next three and a half hours.

By now the children were looking pale, with a dazed and resigned expression on their faces. My girls muttered urgently to me that they needed toilets, and both felt as though they might be sick. The toilet situation in the Ladies Waiting Room wasn't too bad, except that it was hard to pick one's way across the floor in between the sleeping bodies. It was a hole-in-the-floor variety and one of my very sleepy children tried to sit down upon it. I let out a yell that must have waked all the sleeping figures, but it also waked my sleepy daughter.

We returned to our party in time to hear the bad news. There was no Ladies and Gents First-Class Waiting Room.

"But the stationmaster," Ed said, "has given permission

for us to rest in the First-Class Gents Retiring Room."

Loaded down with air mattresses and sleeping bags, we marched to the door of the room and switched on the light. To our surprise and disappointment every seat and bench had someone sleeping on it and none of them looked like First-Class Gents. The only floor space remaining was the corridor leading to the First-Class Gents toilets.

"Well, here we are. It's not much, but it will have to do," said Ed very cheerfully.

"I'm going to be sick," Sarah muttered.

"It's only because you're exhausted," I replied hopefully.

The ten First-Class Gents must have thought that they were having a nightmare, for within seconds four air mattresses had been noisily inflated and laid two by two to form a large and comfortable bed.

"That's all the room there is," said Ed, "so get your sleeping bags, kids, and try and get some rest." All six children managed to curl up somehow on the mattresses and Ang Dooli and I succeeded in wedging ourselves halfway on them as well. During the next three hours I was always conscious of First-Class Gents walking across my legs to the toilet facilities, but Ang Dooli was so exhausted that she was quite oblivious to anything. Max, Lois, and Ed sat patiently on three very upright chairs, and Mike was stretched out like a dead body lying in state on a table in the middle of the room.

All too soon we were told that there was only half an hour before the next train would arrive.

"Up you get, everybody," roared Ed, switching on the light, and the ten First-Class Gents rolled over and eyed us with complete and utter amazement. Pemba Tarkay and Siku came bustling in to deflate the mattresses and roll up the sleeping bags with military precision in front of the incredulous eyes of our audience.

the piles of luggage and, after shaking our hands in very friendly fashion, walked off to find their next train. They were going to Calcutta and must have been very pleased to see the last of us.

It was a clear fresh morning and vendors of fruit and many other foods were setting up their wares on the platform. Everyone seemed bright and cheerful. We counted heads once more and to our relief found all present. There was only one more train to catch—the Assam Mail—leaving in an hour's time for Siliguri in the northern part of West Bengal. The men decided that the women and children should go off and find themselves an omelette for breakfast while they hunted for the right platform for the next train.

The restaurant was clean and efficient and even sported a washbasin and running water. I had brought a little hand towel and soap for such an occasion and we had a good clean-up, while the rest of the clientele of the restaurant watched us with interest. We ordered omelettes for the entire party, but the men didn't have time to eat theirs, so we rolled each omelette in a couple of slices of bread and carried them with us as we ran across an overhead footpath to the waiting Assam Mail. We had reserved seats for this section of the journey and were taken to our correct carriage by an efficient conductor. It was almost too good to be true; we felt most relaxed and happy. The men munched on their omelettes, and we bought fruit and took photographs of our crumpled and worn party.

There was a feeling of victory in the air, for there had been times during the night when we wondered if we would ever reach Siliguri. Now all we had to do was sit on a train for twelve hours. I decided to make the Hillary compartment a little home away from home and unpacked bottles of filtered water, mugs, a towel and some soap, and a large box of food. The tensions of the night had vanished. We waved wildly to all and sundry as the train slid out of the station.

After five minutes, we stopped among the bare fields in the middle of nowhere. The children leaped out of the train and visited each other, and this happened every time we stopped for the rest of the day. Our calls of "Get inside! The train's going to leave!" and "Where are they?" echoed across every station in India.

When the train halted at a sizable town, I realized that Ed's stories of railway travel were at last coming true, for the vendors were calling out their wares in never-ending chorus as they paraded up and down. We were all entranced and rushed to the windows to stare at the various goods that were for sale. "Garam Char" was one of the great favorites with our party. It was sweet, freshly brewed tea sold in little earthenware disposable cups. There were curds, milk, hot water, fruit, biscuits, bread, everything you can imagine on sale. The train stopped every ten or twenty minutes and we spent the day absorbing the fascinating sights of the many and varied stations.

The Indian countryside now looked fertile and productive. We could see crop-covered land stretching away to the horizon, flat and green. Country folk were working in the fields and water buffaloes wallowed in muddy pools. A yellow-saried girl carrying a brass jar of water on her head flashed by, and the hunched backs of working peasants looked peaceful and contented. It was a marvelous way of discovering India, for we were seeing the country people, unaffected by the miseries of city life and of the world elsewhere. At midday the guard came and asked us if we would like to order a meal. Our three children said they would be much happier with stale bread, butter, and salmon from the box of provisions. But we thought it would be a pity if they missed trying an Indian Railway's dinner, so we ordered curry and a glass of tea for everyone. It was a mistake, for the rice was stone cold and the chilies too hot. As we tried to eat the food, scores of beggar boys stood outside the windows with empty tins asking us for leftovers. By the time we had finished our meal there was still a huge pile of rice remaining. I couldn't help wondering what all those hungry people thought of the foreigners who bought so much food and then left at least half of it uneaten. But the food wasn't wasted, for we passed our dishes out through the window, and the Indian children quickly scraped each precious grain of rice into their tins and scampered away from the station.

"Drink up your tea," I said to the children hopefully.

"No, we don't like it," they said. "It's too sweet." I couldn't give away the tea as well, so I poured it out the other side of the train when nobody was looking and then handed the glasses to the waiting railway guard.

During the last couple of hours, our railway journey began to pall. Our eyes were sore from the dust and smoke and too much staring, and we felt cramped and overfed. Mike said he felt ill and decided that he had a stomach infection, but the rest of us agreed that he was suffering from the dozens of cups of tea that he had consumed during the day. As the lights of Siliguri approached and we neared the end of our railway journey, Lois and I decided that we must surely be seasoned travelers by now.

"You know, Lois," I said, "no type of traveling or camping holds any fears for me any longer. If we have to pitch our tents outside the railway station tonight I'll be quite happy."

"I agree," said Lois. "I wouldn't even mind sleeping in another First-Class Gents if I had to." Our boasting and back-slapping continued until the train came to a halt and

we had to make the usual quick move to the platform before being carried on against our will toward Assam.

We had planned to camp at Siliguri, but the idea no
longer seemed so attractive. While the women and children
sat on top of the baggage in the main entrance of the station a couple of the men dashed round town in search of
a hotel. Ed also went off to hunt for alternative accommo-
dations in the station. He disappeared for a long time and
while we waited poor Ang Dooli collapsed in a heap, looking cruelly nauseated. The strange food, low altitude, and
train travel just didn't suit her.

"You children look after Ang Dooli, and the luggage,"
I said, "and Lois and I will go and look for Ed."

"There's nowhere in the station building for us to stay,"
Ed said when we found him, "the place is absolutely
crammed. Everything is going through here for the army
in the Northeast, and anyhow the waiting rooms are
strictly segregated, with lights on everywhere all night."

Max and Mike had been more successful. They'd been
told of a new tourist motel on the outskirts of town, so
we loaded ourselves into three jeeps and set off into the
night. Our taxi man drove in a fanatical fashion and the
vehicle seemed to move along with a crablike motion. It
was thoroughly alarming, as the car lights were pitifully
dim and the streets were pitchy black.

Five hundred yards from the brightly lit entrance of the
new tourist lodge our jeep stopped with a violent jerk.

"Very bad puncture, I'm afraid," said the driver. We all
got out to look and he was certainly right. We must have
been driving on a flat tire for miles.

"We'll walk, thank you," we said very firmly. "Don't worry
about coming any farther."

When our large party arrived outside the office of the

motel, three startled and timid little gentlemen came out
to meet us.

"Can we stay here the night?" we gasped.

"Er, well, some of you can," said the chief spokesman for
the group.

"We are all quite happy to sleep on the floor," I suggested. The hotel looked such a pleasant haven of rest that
I was determined to stay there.

"Well, we must first of all decide what kind of accom-
modations you want," said the manager of the hotel.

"Well, actually we want everything," someone explained.

"But which of you will have what? We have 'A' type
accommodation and 'B1' and 'B2'."

"That's fine," said Ed.

"I will show it to you," said the proud owner. So we
were led from room to room. The first room was large,
plain, and green, with three beds in it, a little dressing room,
and a bathroom. The beds were covered with the most
shiny, steel-colored bedspreads I have ever seen. The next
room was all in salmon pink, with bright pink satin bedspreads and a few incredible pieces of stainless steel
and plastic arts and crafts.

"That must be the honeymoon room," someone suggested.

"That's 'B2' accommodation," corrected our host.

"Oh," we all said intelligently.

Suddenly Max had a bright idea.

"Do you think it would be possible to arrange a light
meal for our party?" he inquired.

"Oh, yes," the trio replied, "but it will take at least half
an hour, for we are not used to catering for such a large
group."

"Just an omelette each and a piece of bread would be
sufficient." I felt as though I had been living on omelettes

and pieces of bread for at least two days, but the thought of food was most pleasant.

"No, you must see Grade 'A' accommodation."

We followed our three guides into a cosy little room with bathroom attached. I can't quite remember the color scheme, but the general impression was of a huge double bed completely covered in a colossal, shiny, mock-tiger skin, red lighting, and a very stuffy atmosphere. "I don't think they can often open up this room," the children whispered.

"Not all that many people would want Grade 'A' accommodation," I told them.

"Let's put Mingma and Ang Dooli in here," Ed said.

Ang Dooli couldn't disguise her joy and threw herself upon the startling bedspread, where she stayed until the next morning. The other three Sherpas quickly set up a cosy camp for themselves on the veranda, and we pumped up air mattresses for our children to sleep on the floor.

"There's hot and cold water," Sarah screamed from the bathroom, "and a shower." But we soon found that no hot water was available.

The hotel staff had to work terribly hard to provide a meal for us and to organize everything, and from the moment we arrived until the next morning when we departed, they never stopped running. They were eager to help in any way, and soon we were all good friends. The evening meal ended up like a relay race, with only six cups, plates, knives, and forks between us. We shared everything as much as we could, but the staff were kept rushing from the kitchen to the dining room with reserve supplies all through the meal. They had to make the toast over an open fire and possessed only one small frying pan for the omelettes, so we took turns in carrying the food to the table and returning the empty plates. There was a one-egg omelette and a

slice of toast apiece, a jar of jam and a few little pats of
butter. We were a ravenous lot and Lois and I tried hard to
pretend we weren't very hungry, as we didn't dare ask
for any more.

The meal finished with a delicious cup of tea drunk
also in relays, due to the lack of cups. The flavor of the
tea was superb, for Siliguri is in the heart of one of the
finest tea-growing areas of India.

"The beds are not made, I'm afraid," said the tired
manager.

"Don't worry," I told him, "we all have sleeping bags
and I've even brought along pillow slips, so we are quite
self-sufficient."

I spent the most blissful and peaceful night that I can
remember for a long time, and woke at 7 A.M., when the
manager brought round a tray of tea. After a breakfast of
the inevitable omelettes and toast, some of the children
went outside to a play area with swings and seesaws. Our
drivers from the night before returned, minus the fanatical one we had paid off. They brought a replacement who
looked a good sensible individual.

At 9 A.M. we were ready to depart, but Tenzing Niendra
was leaving us to travel on to Assam and we steeled ourselves for another sad farewell. When all the good-byes
were over we drove off, waving sadly to the little group—
the tall, strong, and handsome Tenzing Niendra and our
three exhausted hosts who had looked after us so well.
"Those people really deserve to succeed," one of the children said. We all wished them well.

If you are fortunate to pick a lovely clear winter's day for
the drive from Siliguri at nearly sea level up to Darjeeling
at over six thousand feet in the Himalayan foothills, you will
experience one of the loveliest scenic drives in all India.
With our jeeps well laden with luggage and a good supply

of Sikkimese tangerines, we left the outskirts of the town behind but were soon stopped at an army checkpost. All the frontier area of India is heavily patrolled and foreigners must have special permits. A pleasant soldier—clearly a Gurkha hillman—quickly copied down our particulars and handed back our passports. Just as we were about to continue the journey, Ed noticed a little group of army tents across the road. One of the tents had a rainproof-looking fly on it and he asked the checkpost officer if he could take a picture of it. The man looked slightly puzzled, for it is illegal to photograph anything military in India, but this seemed an innocent-enough request.

"I am very interested in designing tents," Ed explained hopefully, and the soldier nodded his permission. Once that was done, we commenced the climb to Darjeeling. First we drove through great forested hills, with fleeting glimpses down onto the plains, and then ground our way upward between neat tea gardens clinging to precipitous slopes. A long and regular line of fruit peelings followed us up the road. Sikkimese oranges are renowned for their sweetness and we competed enthusiastically to eat the last remaining fruit in the bag. Every so often we passed attractive recreation parks that had been set up with shelters and little flower gardens. At Kurseong on the top of the great ridge that leads to Darjeeling, we sounded our horn busily as we drove through narrow little streets bordered by crowded shops, which displayed every type of merchandise, including bright pyramids of oranges. As always, the Tibetan and Sherpa people of the area added to the colorfulness of the scene with their ruddy complexions and graceful clothing.

The standard of living usually rises with the altitude in India, and Kurseong was no exception. Warm clothes and a proper house are a necessity and the people have to work much harder than their lowland brothers to survive. Because of this they appear to be more cheerful and energetic. We were high above the crowded misery of Siliguri and the plains of West Bengal, and what a relief it was!

Our reason for coming to Darjeeling was to stay with Tenzing, Ed's Everest companion of 1953. After leaving the rest of our party safely and very comfortably settled in the attractive Windermere Hotel, we drove off in a terrific hurry to Tenzing's house, where we were expected for lunch. It was wonderful to see Tenzing again, looking as fit and handsome as ever, and great fun to meet his beautiful wife, Daku, and their three small children. Tenzing's grown-up daughter, Pem Pem, who has three children of her own, was there to welcome us also. Tenzing had decided we would enjoy some European food, so when we were comfortably settled around the large dining room table, Daku served a huge meal of roast chicken, roast potatoes, cauliflower in white sauce, and spinach. We ate ravenously. The plates were then cleared away and Tenzing told us we were to have some Indian curry as well. We wondered how we would ever eat another large course, but the curry and fried rice were so delicious that we stuffed ourselves to the bursting point.

Tenzing's large house was a collector's showplace, filled with Sherpa and Tibetan handicrafts. The floors and the seating were covered with beautiful traditional carpets, many of them incredibly fine. Tenzing told us with great pride that some of them had been bought in Lhasa thirty years before for a few rupees. In his living room were red lacquered pieces of furniture decorated with bright Tibetan designs, while upstairs on the third floor was a treasure-filled private chapel.

Tenzing and Daku are both Sherpas and originally came

from the village of Thami in the Everest region of Nepal. Ed had met Daku's parents on quite a few occasions when he was working on the Thami school.

After unpacking a few of our belongings, we were taken down the hill to the Darjeeling bazaar and the brisk walk in the mountain air soon helped digest our meal. There were very few customers among the stalls and our children had the chance to see the spices, strange vegetables, and fruits in comparative peace. The highlight of the tour was a visit to an Indian sweet shop. Our two guides bought a large boxful of every type of Indian sweetmeat and we stood in the middle of the bazaar taking bites out of everything and passing it on to someone else. Indian sweets are mostly made of sugar and milk and are sickeningly sweet to our palates. By the time we had finished our sampling we all began to wonder what was going to happen to our overtaxed stomachs. The energetic hill climb back to Tenzing's house soon took care of that, and we were ready for whatever entertainments the evening was to bring.

Tenzing still had two more social engagements for us that day. At 6 P.M. we were bidden to cocktails at the home of Colonel Kumar, principal of the Himalayan Mountaineering Institute, and we spent a pleasant couple of hours meeting and talking with the staff. The Institute was founded after Tenzing and Ed climbed Everest in 1953. Pandit Nehru decided that a climbing school organized along the same lines as an Outward Bound School would be beneficial to the younger Indian generation, and, very sensibly, he decided that Tenzing should be used as the senior instructor and dominating personality of the institution. The Himalayan Mountaineering Institute has been in operation for thirteen years and has taught hundreds of young men and women the basic skills and joys of outdoor living. Many young people from the plains have learned to toughen themselves physically and mentally at the Institute and we could sense the feeling of confidence and competence that had resulted in an Indian expedition reaching the top of Mount Everest.

Already behind schedule, we were dragged away by Tenzing to a family dinner party arranged in our honor. The jeep drove down the quiet and darkened streets of Darjeeling to a little Tibetan restaurant just above the bazaar. Here we were met by several of Tenzing's closest relatives and were escorted into a cosy dining room by four burly, grinning Tibetans.

"You are going to have a truly Tibetan dinner tonight," Tenzing said. It must have been at least 8 P.M. and our three children were looking rather tired, but during the next three hours they coped with chopsticks and the interminable meal like seasoned travelers. I was never more proud of them.

Once we were seated, Tibetan tea complete with yak butter and salt was served. Then great bowls of rice and many different currylike dishes were put in front of us. There were mixtures of different types of meats, vegetables, fish, and noodles, most of them heavily seasoned with chili. We sampled the food with great interest, but after the sixth dish my appetite began to flag.

"Ooh, this one's good," said Sarah, trying a curry of chicken and bright red chilies. I sat and stared at her in fascination as she crunched up a few pieces of chili and chicken without so much as a gasp for air or a scream for a glass of water. Peter was equally adventurous and tackled every dish with the most amazing capacity. Then came a lull in the proceedings as hunks of Tibetan bread were offered to us. This was a refreshing and beneficial change of diet and I ate a large cake-sized piece. The bread looked as though it had been made like Scottish damper in a large, heavy container over an open fire. But it was only a brief respite, for soon six more dishes were brought in for us to sample. We ate on and on. It's amazing how much you can swallow as long as you take it slowly.

At 10:30 P.M. Tenzing announced we had eaten sixteen courses and that there were two more to come but he had decided to cancel them. Even his experienced relations didn't seem too disappointed about this, and we completed the meal by cleansing our jaded palates with oranges.

"We'll have to walk home, as there's no transport so late at night," said Tenzing. This suited us perfectly, as a walk in the bracing air was exactly what we needed. The four huge, smiling Tibetans bowed us out of their restaurant and we hurried home. Ang Puri, a sweet little Sherpa girl of fifteen, was filling our hot water bottles as we entered the house.

"Where does Ang Puri come from?" I asked Tenzing.

"Oh she comes from Thami. You probably remember her father, a little man called Nami. He had been drinking too much rakshi, so I took Ang Puri and her sister and gave them a home here. They help Daku in the house and I send them to school."

The Tenzing household seemed to be filled with young people he was looking after for somebody else. There were at least six of them being educated, fed, and financed in this way. We were deeply impressed with all that Tenzing was doing for his Sherpa people, for until he was over forty he had been by most standards a poor man. Now that his financial position had improved he was quite willing to spend some of his wealth on his less fortunate friends and relations.

Next morning I thought I was still dreaming when Daku

floated into our room to announce that breakfast would be ready at 8 A.M. She looked so beautiful that it just took my breath away. Her shiny black hair was arranged in a graceful thick plait reaching to her waist, and her rich olive complexion and bright rosy cheeks contrasted superbly with her brown tunic and vivid sky-blue blouse. Ed decided then and there that he would trade me in for a new and younger wife.

Our host and hostess were determined to give us a wonderful last day in Darjeeling. Immediately after breakfast we started with a tour of the Himalayan Mountaineering Institute. Everyone clicked their cameras furiously at Mount Kanchenjunga, which floated magnificently above a sea of clouds some thirty or forty miles away.

"We are going to let you have a go at Tenzing's Rock," said Colonel Kumar. A few minutes later we stopped on the road below the Institute, where a great smooth chunk of rock reached out over the valley. The first person to climb it was Tenzing's little chubby five-year-old son, who scrambled quite easily to the top with his father. "Of course, there are many more difficult routes up the rock," Colonel Kumar said, "and during every mountaineering course students come down here to train." Ed pretended he didn't hear about the more difficult routes and took Peter and Belinda up by the easy way.

We then drove on to the Darjeeling Tibetan Self-Help Center, which has largely been organized by one of the sisters of the Dalai Lama and has become famous for its excellent Tibetan carpets. We were shown a great pile of beautiful carpets and lost our hearts to a couple of them. But alas, we were told we would have to put our names on a waiting list. Feeling rather deflated, we decided to forget the whole thing and went for a quick tour of the center. The Tibetans operate a nursery for their babies and this was one of Tenzing's particular interests. The babies had just been fed and were now resting, so we were ushered into a room filled with about fifty cots, each containing a small black-haired, red-cheeked person tucked neatly under a brightly colored quilt. It was the most cuddly and contented sight that I have ever seen. The large, comfortable Tibetan woman in charge smiled patiently at us, and her little charges slept on during our rather noisy visit.

Horses were then produced as if by magic, and our three children rode joyously back into town while the rest of us followed by car.

"We must leave for Kalimpong straight after lunch," I said to Tenzing.

"Of course you shall, don't worry. Straight after lunch," he replied.

By 4 P.M., lunch was finished and we sadly packed our belongings and ourselves into three overladen jeeps. As a final thoughtful gesture, a large bag of oranges was thrust onto our laps.

"Good-bye," we yelled.

"Come back soon," they called.

"Of course we will," we replied rather sadly, knowing it might be years before we could return.

"Traveling is just one long emotional upheaval," I said to Ed. "Every parting just tears you apart and we've been having partings for weeks."

"How about eating an orange?" said Ed.

CHAPTER 18

Farewell Himalayas

···

Down the steep and twisting road we hurtled, passing through all the different vegetation levels. Fir trees, tea gardens, and tropical jungles flashed by while our driver pumped at the footbrakes furiously and a red warning light kept flashing on and off on the instrument panel.

"These Darjeeling drivers are really terrific," said Ed. "They can cope with any road and they are excellent mechanics as well."

"Are they good at crash landings also?" I inquired, looking at the ominous warning light. To my surprise, I wasn't told to eat another orange.

Safely down in the humid atmosphere of the Teesta river we were stopped by another army checkpost. We were now very close to Sikkim and the Tibetan border and the Teesta bridge was an important link in the communications between the Indian soldiers patrolling the frontier and the rest of India.

We handed in our permits and bought another bag of oranges to replace our dwindling supplies, then drove over the bridge and up the steep hillside toward Kalimpong. The road was nearly as steep as the one we had just descended, but it faced the sun and poinsettias and bright golden creepers were still blooming in profusion beside the road.

Kalimpong is peaceful and charming and much warmer than Darjeeling, for it is at an altitude of only four thousand feet. The winter climate is superb, with brilliant, clear, sunny days and only a very light frost at night. Its population consists of a fascinating collection of different races and nationalities—Tibetans, Bhutanese, Sikkimese, Indians, Sherpas, Nepalese, and so on. But the most wonderful people in Kalimpong are the famous McDonald sisters, who run the Himalayan Hotel—Mrs. Vicki Williams, Mrs. Annie Perry, and Miss Vera McDonald. Apart from a large share of Scottish and Tibetan blood, their racial background is as mixed as the entire population of Kalimpong. Their father was a British Trade Agent in Tibet for many years and because of this the sisters are special friends to all the Tibetan refugees of the area. They are also friends of everyone who lives in Kalimpong and of all the guests lucky enough to stay in their hotel. It's hardly a hotel, just a big comfortable family home, and when the Hillarys, Pearls, Mike Gill, and their Sherpa friends descended upon them, we filled their house to bursting point.

Vicki Williams has organized all the teaching staff for our Sherpa schools in Nepal, and when she saw our four Sherpa companions she made them doubly welcome. Poor Ang Dooli was still suffering from traveling and strange food and they treated her with such tender care that she very soon recovered. Vera presided over the kitchen department at the hotel and she had special Tibetan food cooked for Ang Dooli each day, to build up her strength and morale.

Every Saturday in Kalimpong there is a market day, The Hart. It's the gayest and most colorful market. We wandered round the busy stalls, being careful not to trip over merchandise that had been laid out on the footpath for want of a better place. I was drawn like a magnet to the little stalls filled with odd bits and pieces, where I bought rough brown sealing wax that looked like dehydrated sausages and a necklace made of squares of cheese threaded on string. There were little white pats of dried yeast for making beer. The yeast had been dried on fern leaves and underneath each portion was a delightful green pattern. I bought some of these to take back to New Zealand. One of the most important items on my shopping list was incense for the copper incense burner I had bought from the monk at Seti Gompa. The Sherpa people use a mixture of dried azalea and juniper leaves and I was able to purchase a large bundle wrapped up in newspaper.

The children had been saving some money for Kalimpong and now they had their turn. All of them wanted a Kukhri, the fearsome Gurkha knife, and we were able to buy some bloodthirsty models for only five rupees each. The woolen goods were so cheap and well made that both families bought great bundles of homespun handknitted socks for two or three rupees a pair. I obtained a turtle-necked homespun jersey for Peter and it cost only eighteen rupees.

In this bright and relatively prosperous atmosphere, Ang Dooli's clothes looked a little worn and faded, so Ed and I took her aside and bought her a pink cardigan, which suited her rosy cheeks perfectly. She was very thrilled and when it was all wrapped up, she gave it to Mingma to hold. A little later in our wanderings through the bazaar Ang Dooli disappeared but returned after a few minutes accompanied by the Pearls. She was proudly holding another cardigan, bright green in hue, that the Pearls had given her, not knowing of our recent purchase. We all thought it was a great joke, except for Mingma, who was very angry with Ang Dooli.

"Don't worry Mingma," we said. "We've all been wanting to give Ang Dooli some presents for a long time."

We left the market area and walked up the hill to a street that is known as the Tenth Mile. The Tibetans have settled in great numbers here and run the most intriguing little shops filled with Tibetan clothes and household necessities. For six weeks Sarah had been talking about getting a Sherpa dress, and as Sherpa and Tibetan clothes are identical this seemed the place to do it. We entered the first little shop accompanied by half a dozen inquisitive and friendly Tibetans. I told the shopkeeper that I wanted clothes for the three children and immediately the Tibetans started giving advice and making suggestions until we were completely baffled. Before we knew what had happened, many helpful hands had dressed our children in little Tibetan outfits. Sarah and Belinda each wore a black bhaku (tunic) and a brightly colored blouse and sash, while Peter looked very dashing in a long-sleeved bhaku and green sash. Eager helpers smoothed down the girls' gowns and a large crowd gathered to admire the finished products. A handsome Tibetan matron tied Sarah's sash so tightly that the child looked at me with horror and said she couldn't breathe. The complete sets of clothing cost eighteen rupees each and Belinda and Peter walked triumphantly home wearing their new clothes, while Sarah, who was a bit more self-conscious, carried hers shyly in a parcel. By the end of the day all six children were dressed in Tibetan clothes and they looked so pretty and so pleased with themselves that everyone we met in Kalimpong looked quite delighted also.

Our three days in Kalimpong were very happy ones and we were lulled into a pleasant, lethargic state by the peace and beauty that surrounded us. In front of the hotel was a graceful white camellia tree and a sheltered lawn bordered by giant white daisy bushes. Here we sat in comfort under an exotic Tibetan awning and let the days go by. We stared across the deep valleys toward the distant snow peaks of Tibet and listened to the busy sounds of the town drifting up from below.

On the night before our departure for Calcutta, Vera Mc-Donald produced my children's favorite Kalimpong dinner, which they had nicknamed "Himalayan Hamburgers" (mincemeat inside potato). Afterward, we sat beside a cosy charcoal brazier, surrounded by Tibetan and Chinese treasures of a bygone era, and sipped cautiously at a Bhutanese liqueur named imaginatively "Liquid Gold." All too soon it was nearly midnight and we had to go upstairs and pack our belongings for yet another departure.

In the dark shivering hours of the next morning a collection of old vehicles came chugging up to the front door of the Himalayan Hotel. The females of the party were instructed to get into a dignified and ancient Dodge minibus. Peter, Ed, and Max climed into a jeep piled high with luggage, and Mike and the three Sherpas wedged themselves in another. More sad good-byes followed and then we rattled and banged out the gate and through the quiet town. As we corkscrewed our way toward the Teesta river, mighty Kanchenjunga loomed up across the valley, its summit tipped with a red sunrise. All the way down the long hill, fumes seeped up through the many cracks and crannies in the floor of our old vehicle and by the time we reached the Teesta bridge everybody looked a little pale.

"Well, it's not quite so twisty from now on, surely," said Lois hopefully. "We'll keep all the windows open and we should be all right."

"What say somebody feels sick?" said Sarah, who obviously was. "How do we tell the driver? He doesn't speak any English."

"Don't worry," I replied, "I could probably say it in Nepali, but I think it will be perfectly obvious."

The road continued to twist and turn for a while, and it wasn't until we were half an hour from Siliguri that we caught sight of the other vehicles. The jeep containing our husbands had been waiting for us but now carried on ahead. We watched its progress with mesmerized and hysterical disbelief. The whole canvas roof seemed to have come loose and it flapped crazily in the breeze like one in an old Charlie Chaplin movie. This wouldn't have mattered too much but their driver seemed to have no control over the steering and they progressed down the road in a wild and weaving fashion. Every time an oncoming car approached, they had to stop for fear of having a collision. For some unknown reason, Lois and I never became genuinely concerned about our husbands, for the antics of the jeep seemed so unreal that it was impossible to believe it could in any way affect us.

We shot past Siliguri and carried on the few extra miles to Bagdogra Airport. Everyone became unnaturally quiet as we unloaded our gear and checked our tickets for the flight to Calcutta. The imminent departure of our great friends Pemba Tarkay and Siku was affecting us considerably, and it was Ed who finally broke the depressing silence and succeeded in making us face up to the inevitable.

"Now, Siku and Pemba Tarkay," he said, "you must drive back in one of the jeeps to Siliguri and get on the train tonight for Raxaul. I think it would be a good idea if you went right now."

"Let's go and see them off," we said to one another, trying to be terribly cheerful. So outside we went, to be presented with scarves in the most depressing of ceremonies. Poor Siku and Pemba Tarkay looked as though they were going to burst with emotion, and we all gulped and choked as we said our final words of farewell.

"Off you go now," said Ed in a stifled sort of voice, and we stood and watched as the jeep disappeared down the road. We returned sadly to the airport building and had our passports checked while the five girls sat in a line with tears trickling down their faces.

In just over two hours we were walking wearily and limply across the tarmac of Dum Dum Airport in Calcutta. A suicidal driver whisked us to the heart of the city and all five of us squashed into one large air-conditioned hotel room. Calcutta is no place for children, but we had to spend a day there to arrange the shipping of scientific gear back to New Zealand. Our holiday was finished, and the charm and excitement of travel and adventure had completely disappeared. All I wanted to do was get on a plane and head for home, but there was still enough time left for Peter and me to find ourselves in the middle of an unexpected and alarming incident.

We had been searching for Indian raw silk in the bazaar and when the time came for us to return to our hotel, there was not a taxi anywhere in sight. The only available transport was a rickshaw, but I have always abhorred the rickshaws of Asia, as I do not approve of sitting on a little seat and being pulled by a fellow human. The streets were filled with a jostling throng and my feet felt hot and tired. Finally, shrugging off my scruples with the excuse that I would be giving some poor devil a chance to earn some money, I hailed a rickshaw. Our rickshaw man was obviously bent on self-destruction, for instead of jogging peacefully along the side of the road he rushed headlong into the center of the dense traffic. The buses had such swarms of people clinging to the side entrances that they leaned over in the most unstable fashion. At one stage Peter and I were sandwiched between four of these great leaning monsters and we felt that death was imminent. To make matters worse, I think we were a bit too heavy, and I felt as if the rickshaw would fall over backward. When we had got ourselves stuck in a maze of overladen rush-hour traffic, our astonishing rickshaw man decided that he wanted to change direction against this overwhelming tide of humanity.

"Where are you going?" I screamed shrilly. But I was wasting my breath.

"Oh, Mum, this is terrible," said Peter.

"Yes, it is, but there's nothing we can do. If we get out of the rickshaw now, we'll be killed for certain."

By some miracle we found ourselves safely in a quiet side street, but not satisfied with that experience our man started running along toward some fearfully overcrowded crossroads.

"Enough! Enough!" I yelled, but he took no notice. We sailed royally across the intersection while bus drivers shook their fists at us and cars tooted alarmingly on all sides. We continued at great speed down a tree-lined road that certainly didn't lead to our hotel.

"Right! Get ready to jump," I said to Peter. "He's obviously trying to lose us or cheat us."

"Stop! Stop!" I yelled even louder, and finally I made myself heard. We stopped and both scrambled down onto solid earth. I recognized where we were, and realized that despite our long and frightening experiences we had barely traveled one city block.

"Here's a rupee."

"Five rupees," he replied.

"What nonsense, we only paid the taxi a rupee to get us to the bazaar in the first place."

"But I am a human, Memsahib, and not a machine."

"That may be true," I said, "but you've taken us round and round, getting us nowhere." It was an unpleasant situation, for I would gladly have given the man ten rupees except he had tried to cheat and frighten us. In the end I paid him three rupees, while an interested little crowd gathered round to watch the fun.

We crossed over another road to some little shops on the side of the footpath, and there sitting cross-legged on the grubby Calcutta street was Ang Dooli trying on a new pair of sandals.

"Only three rupees!" she called out.

"They're the same as the ones you bought me, Mum," said Peter. Ang Dooli grinned with pleasure.

"How much were yours, Peter?" inquired the careful Mingma.

"Fifteen rupees," said Peter. We all laughed.

"It's just no good," I said. "People like us don't stand a chance in Calcutta."

For the last couple of days there had been a nagging sadness at the back of our minds when we remembered how soon we would have to say good-bye to Mingma and Ang Dooli. The daughterless Ang Dooli had completely fallen in love with Belinda and Belinda loved her dearly. During the last two weeks of travel they had been constant companions, and in Calcutta they had held hands to protect one another from the wicked city.

"Ang Dooli is my other mother," said Belinda with deep conviction.

We drove to Dum Dum Airport along the big new highway which all Calcutta taxi drivers think of as a racetrack, and by the time we reached our destination we were all in a state of extreme nervous exhaustion.

While we waited for our flight to be called, Ang Dooli sat with Belinda on her lap and the tears poured down her cheeks. The rest of us sat facing her, feeling strained and dejected. Then over the loudspeaker came the terrible tidings that our flight had been delayed half an hour. This was absolute torture. The half hour dragged on minute by minute, until mercifully we were told to go through Customs and Mingma and Ang Dooli were given special permission to come through with us. No one could speak as we exchanged scarves and hugged each other desperately. The tears welled up in our eyes as the memories of our happy months together came flooding back. Even the stoutest heart would have found it impossible to cover up his feelings. But as our two most special friends were gently led away from us a most incongruous incident occurred. The entire Customs staff of the airport chose this emotion-packed moment to come and shake the Hero of Everest by the hand. Not content with just meeting "Sir Hillary" they presented themselves to the entire party and looked so happy and pleased with life that there was nothing for it but to pull ourselves together and smile back. As soon as it was possible to leave the friendly group, we rushed as fast as we could across the unbearably hot tarmac to the waiting plane and fell into our seats with intense relief. The next few minutes passed swiftly as we relaxed, lost in our own private reveries. Then we were airborne and winging our way across the Hooghly river toward Bangkok and New Zealand, while thousands of feet below, Mingma and Ang Dooli watched us disappear. Far out to our left a ghostly bank of clouds sailed above the thick haze of the hot plains of India. Somewhere among those clouds were the towering Himalayas—timeless, peaceful, and glorious. No wonder the people of Asia believe they are the home of the Gods.

The abrupt change of scene lifted us out of our despondency, and thoughts of home started to dominate our children's minds.

"Four more days and you'll be back at school," I teased.

"I can't remember a thing," said Ann. "How do you say, 'Thank you,' in French?"

"Oh, I don't know," said Lynn and Peter.

"How do you say, 'Thank you,' in Nepali?" I asked.

"Dhanyabad," they all chorused back.

"How do you say, 'Thank you,' in Sherpa?"

"Tuchi."

And "Tuchi che" (thank you very much), all you wonderful and very dear Sherpa people, for your friendship and hospitality, and thank you very much, all you other friends in Nepal and India, for this unforgettable Himalayan holiday.